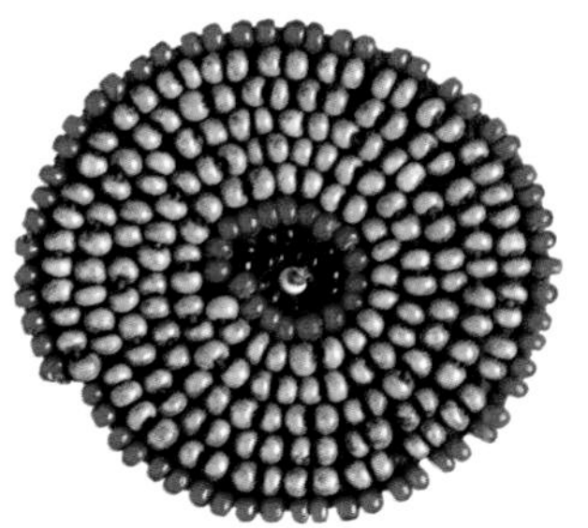

SOUTH-EAST AFRICAN BEADWORK
1850-1910
FROM ADORNMENT TO ARTEFACT TO ART

SOUTH EAST AFRICAN BEADWORK

1850-1910

FROM ADORNMENT TO ARTEFACT TO ART

EDITED BY MICHAEL STEVENSON
AND MICHAEL GRAHAM-STEWART
WITH AN INTRODUCTORY ESSAY
BY SANDRA KLOPPER

Fernwood Press
P O Box 15344
8018 Vlaeberg

Registration no. 90/04463/07

First published 2000

Design by Gillian Fraenkel (gillf@cinet.co.za)
Cover design by Willem Jordaan
Reproduction by Cape Imaging Bureau (Cape Town) CC
Printed and bound by Tien Wah Press (Pte) Ltd, Singapore

ISBN 1 874950 52 0

Michael Graham-Stewart
173 Bond Street
London W1Y 9PB
e-mail: mgs173@msn.com

Michael Stevenson
P O Box 45066
7735 Claremont
Cape Town
e-mail: michael@michaelstevenson.com

Contents

Preface

African Bank Investments Limited values its association with this project to repatriate southern African beadwork from abroad, a century or more after it was taken from this region. Unfortunately, a significant portion of the beadwork of the period that has survived is in collections in Europe because very few families here were in a position to pass beadwork down the generations as most South Africans' life histories were disrupted by apartheid. Over the years the museums in southern Africa have accumulated collections of beadwork, and more recently the art galleries have sought out individual pieces. But these institutions have seldom had the resources to systematically collect and display beadwork in a manner appropriate to its importance in the history of art and culture in the subcontinent. We as a company are privileged to accept the role as guardians for future generations of material pieces in the book, and anticipate that our collection and the exhibitions of it will contribute to a wider understanding and appreciation of this art form. Through this effort we are also hopeful that the role and contribution of African women to the development of South African art takes its rightful place.

The tradition of making beadwork in South Africa survived in spite of the fact that the fabric of our society was undermined in the past century. Beadwork remains a vibrant living tradition, with recent beadwork incorporating current fashions and designs and adapting to the tastes of our time. The late 19th-century pieces illustrated in this book stand as a testimony to the creative spirit of the unidentified African women whose skills and talents in the past produced extraordinary pieces. So few of our generation have seen such pre-1900 works which are the root of contemporary beadwork. We are of the hope that beadworkers and other artists in looking to the future can draw inspiration from these historical pieces. As a bank that fosters a philosophy of growth, we view this association and our support for art and heritage in this country as an integral component of our holistic approach to ensuring the economic and social wellbeing of South African art.

African Bank Investments Limited

Foreword

The collection illustrated here had its modest origin more than a decade ago, when we bought various pieces of south-east African beadwork with appealing designs. As we set about researching each particular piece, we were always astonished at how little is known about beadwork from this region. The focus of African art collecting has been on 'traditional' figurative pieces, and more recently interest has extended to material culture, textiles and costume. But pieces, such as beadwork, which are not made entirely from indigenous material, and are on occasions made expressly for sale, fall outside these categories, and thus tend to remain neglected. It is for this reason that we decided to publish our collection, which should go some way towards sensitising art historians, collectors and curators to the extraordinary breadth of the field, and the complexity and nuances in the designs of late 19th- and early 20th-century beadwork from south-east Africa. The many comparisons that can be made between pieces in this book and those in other collections should, with time, assist researchers in refining the classification of beadwork from this particular area and period, and ensure that it is better understood.

Unfortunately this is not a comprehensive survey of all south-east African beadwork because collectors in the second half of the 19th and early 20th centuries focused on North Nguni beadwork from the Colony of Natal and the Zulu kingdom. This bias is reflected in this book, although we have sought out pieces from the South Nguni, Sotho, and Yao, and the other groups of people who also produced beadwork at this time in south-east Africa. But there are pieces illustrated in paintings by 19th-century South African artists, such as Frederick Timpson I'Ons and Thomas Baines, which we have never seen in reality, and this poses the question whether any of these pieces were collected at the time and if so, whether they will reappear at some point in the future. It should also be borne in mind that our selection has been primarily guided by the age, aesthetic appeal and condition of each piece, rather than by any ethnographic or anthropological considerations.

This book has been compiled with the assistance of numerous people. We would like to acknowledge the cooperation of Sandra Klopper, who wrote the introductory essay and the captions for the illustrations in the essay section. We would also like to thank Guy Tillim and his assistant Megan Tjasink who photographed the beadwork, Gillian Fraenkel who patiently and sensitively designed the layout for the book, Jackie Loos for assisting with picture research, Dee Nash for helping with editing, Joan Hutchinson who conserved the pieces, Deon Viljoen for his advice, Hanno de Swardt and Nellie Pigot for their support, and Marjory van der Merwe, Petros Sethoa, Julia Teale and Steven Long who all in different ways assisted with cataloguing.

Michael Stevenson & Michael Graham-Stewart

1

Plate 1: Two Xhosa-speaking women photographed in a studio in Port Elizabeth in the late 19th century. The practice of wearing beaded breast coverings of this kind was comparatively common both among Xhosa-speaking groups like the Bomvana and some of their Sotho-speaking neighbours. These beaded garments, which commonly reached to the knee, were worn only on festive occasions. More generally, women wore breast-cloths sewn either from leather or from imported cloth.

Although most breast-covers were made from large white beads, in some areas, like Herschel, they were sewn from blue beads, while in Lesotho they were made from blue and black or white beads. Unlike the comparatively small beaded aprons also worn by married women from the eastern Cape, these breast-cloths were not woven into beadwork tapestries. This may be ascribed to the fact that people presumably enjoyed the kinetic visual effects created by the loose beaded fronds during dance sequences.

See no. 1 for a similar breast-cover

Printed on reverse: 'From the studio of G. F. Williams. Artist & Photographer. Port Elizabeth'

Photograph: Michael Graham-Stewart collection

From adornment to artefact to art: historical perspectives on south-east African beadwork

Sandra Klopper

'The merchandise with which we were supplied was exposed, but out of the whole stock he [Molihaban, king of the Bechuana] selected only beads. It was agreed that for an ox should be given two pounds of fine glass and porcelain beads of various colours, or three pounds of small white, blue, green, red, or yellow beads, or three and a half pounds of large blue and white glass beads (the value of about four rixdollars, fifteen shillings sterling); to the knives they objected, as cutting only on one side, whilst theirs were sharp on both; to the tinder-boxes and steels, because they themselves produced fire by the friction of two pieces of wood; to looking-glasses, as being of no use; to handkerchiefs, as not being so strong as their leather caps.'

P.B. Borcherds, *An auto-biographical memoir*, Cape Town, 1861, p.63

As this quote from the memoirs of one of the members of the Somerville and Truter expedition to the Bechuana people in 1801 illustrates, beads were a primary means of exchange in southern Africa prior to the large-scale European colonisation of the region. Beads consequently played a significant role in the ever-changing relations between earlier Arab, and later European traders and the black communities they encountered throughout the southern African region. Mostly in the late 19th century, travellers, missionaries and colonial agents also collected the beadwork produced by these communities as curios and souvenirs. It is from such surviving pieces that the present collection has been assembled. Ultimately, therefore, this collection reflects the social and aesthetic interests not only of the people who made these items of adornment, but also those who acquired them in the field.

The re-emergence and sale of this beadwork, mainly by the descendants of British families with South African connections, highlights a further aspect of this history: the gradual reclassification of various types of objects of African manufacture, first from curio to artefact, and, more recently, from artefact to art.[1] For a number of reasons, the transformation of beadwork into collectable art objects has been comparatively slow, however. Until quite recently, collectors have concentrated on acquiring household and other objects carved from wood, and it has, generally, only been large public institutions that have purchased beadwork for their collections.

In South Africa, this gradual reclassification of beadwork into art is clearly underlined by the comparatively recent acquisition of beadwork pieces by galleries formerly concerned to collect the 'fine arts' of painting, sculpture and drawing. The latter trend was pioneered by the committee appointed to buy works for the Standard Bank Foundation Collection of African Art, which has been housed in the Gertrude Postel Gallery at the University of the Witwatersrand since 1979.[2] Other, publically funded galleries, including the Johannesburg Art

2

Plate 2: Two 'Fingo swells' with beaded tobacco pouches. Pouches of this kind, which were used for carrying matches, pipes and personal tobacco supplies, were beaded in a number of different ways.

Throughout the eastern Cape, Xhosa-speaking communities also wore beaded capes or blankets. Originally made from leather, these indigenously manufactured garments were gradually replaced by blankets obtained in exchange (mainly) for cattle and ivory. Even after the 1830s, when expanding trade relations led to a decline in the value of beads in this region, the beaded decorations found on these garments remained quite sparse, presumably in part for aesthetic reasons, but probably also because the addition of large quantities of beads would have made a significant difference to their weight. The decorative details found on these blankets varied considerably from one region to another.
See nos. 2–7 for similar bags and nos. 33–35 for blankets
Photograph: Michael Graham-Stewart collection

Gallery and the South African National Gallery in Cape Town, were soon to follow, possibly as much for ideological reasons as for any real concern to celebrate the aesthetic qualities of this art form. The two most significant local exhibitions of southern African art, the *Art and ambiguity* show held at the Johannesburg Art Gallery in 1991 and the *Ezakwantu: Beadwork from the Eastern Cape* show held at the South African National Gallery in 1993, both followed the unbanning of the African National Congress and other political organisations in early 1990.[3]

However, widespread aesthetic interest in the beadwork traditions of southern Africa first emerged in the course of the 1970s, when several Johannesburg-based dealers started collecting large quantities of 20th-century pieces in the field. Initially, this interest in local beadwork was restricted almost entirely to the Ndebele, probably because the works produced by Ndebele women consist mainly of large, flat beaded panels and blankets that can readily be displayed as works of art.[4] In the course of the 1980s, this interest in Ndebele beadwork also led to the publication of a number of texts that sought to underline and celebrate the beauty of the beaded blankets and other beadwork items made by this group, notably Knight and Priebatsch's *Ndebele images* (1983) and Courtney-Clarke's *Ndebele: The art of an African tribe* (1986). But the growing aesthetic interest in beadwork that gave rise to these and several shorter publications on the Ndebele[5] was soon to spread to other areas in the region, especially the south-eastern seaboard formerly dominated by the Zulu kingdom, where many beadwork traditions still survive to this day.

Most of the older beadwork items that appeared on the international market in the course of the 1980s originated from the latter region, rather than among the Ndebele and other groups further north. Two reasons may be cited for the lack of old Ndebele pieces to enter the secondary market. Firstly, even if Ndebele beadwork had been available, it would have been very difficult to collect early examples of beadwork produced by this group for the simple but important reason that Ndebele families were indentured to white farmers following the Mapoch War of 1883. Scattered across the Transvaal highveld, they became more or less invisible until the 1930s when they started producing distinctive wall decorations.[6] Secondly, and more importantly, it was only after the 1883 war that this group first adopted the practice of making beadwork on a large scale, probably as a direct response to the experience of being indentured.[7] Like the subsequent emergence among the Ndebele of distinctive forms of wall decoration, these beadwork traditions appear to have been embraced in a deliberate attempt both to declare and to reaffirm a sense of group cohesion.

Plate 3: Like many other 19th-century photographs of Zulu-speakers, this image was taken on one of the black locations established in the Colony of Natal in 1846–47, a decision which led to the relocation of nearly 80 000 people. Notable for the variety of beadwork patterns and colours worn by the women depicted in it, this photograph also includes a pregnancy apron made from the skin of a wild buck. As the apron recorded here indicates, these garments were commonly studded with brass beads made by indigenous metalsmiths from imported ingots. The use of dress to underline different stages in the lives of women (and men) is evidenced further in the fringed aprons – made from the underskin of the leaves of the ubendle *plant – worn by two of the young unmarried women included in this photograph. Like the skirts that girls appear to have worn before the rise to power of the first Zulu king, Shaka, which included a small skin fringe, these* ubendle *leaf skirts were gradually replaced either with beaded cotton skirts, or beaded pubic aprons like the one worn here by the second young woman standing from the left.*
Imprinted: 'Barnett'
Photograph: Michael Graham-Stewart collection

Early collectors

Throughout southern Africa, 19th-century collecting practices obviously depended entirely on indigenous patterns of bead consumption, which varied considerably from one area to another. Along the south-east African coast, where most communities were in direct contact with white traders, beads were generally acquired in much larger quantities than in areas further inland. There is, in fact, considerable evidence to suggest that some communities living in this region started acquiring beads even before the emergence of the Zulu kingdom in the early 19th century.[8]

The acquisition of beadwork in some areas rather than others was further influenced by the comparative ease with which outsiders were able to gain access to certain communities. Large quantities of 19th- and early 20th-century beadwork presumably were collected in present-day KwaZulu-Natal mainly because the indigenous groups living in this region were never dispersed: even after the Zulu kingdom had been destroyed by British forces in 1879, its people continued to occupy huge tracts of land formerly under the control of Shaka and his successors.

As early as the mid-19th century, white travellers who visited the newly proclaimed Colony of Natal to the south of the Zulu kingdom had the exciting option of experiencing Zulu life at first hand by visiting one of the 'native locations' set up in the vicinity of Durban, i.e. the Port Natal region. Established towards the end of the 1840s to consolidate the territories occupied by Africans residing in the colony, these locations made it easier both to preach to and to police the indigenous groups living to the south of the Thukela river.[9] Here, one could encounter people dressed almost entirely in beadwork, and perhaps purchase a piece or two to take or send home to Britain. In contrast to people from the Zulu kingdom, these Zulu-speaking communities had been actively excluded from the benefits of the Delagoa Bay trade in the 18th and early 19th centuries.[10] Many of them were further impoverished by Shaka and his immediate successor Dingane, who demanded tribute in the form of cattle, furs and feathers from their southern neighbours. Once these marginalised communities began to supply the needs of the new white colony in the mid-19th century, however, they soon acquired beads in large quantities, leading to the development of richly varied beadwork styles.[11]

Circumstantial evidence suggests that by far the majority of the 19th-century beadwork pieces that are now entering the market were collected from the black locations occupied by these Zulu-speaking communities. Because several of the Natal 'native locations' initially were controlled by missionaries working for the American Board of Commissioners, a considerable number of beadwork items from this region later entered public collections in the USA. Among these is the Grout collection, possibly the earliest collection of beadwork from south-east Africa, which is now in Vermont and which almost certainly came from the Colony of Natal rather than the Zulu kingdom. (Lewis Grout was stationed from 1847 to 1862

4

Plate 4: Jemima Blackburn's Meeting the Zulus in London *depicts several performers involved in an 1853 exhibition at St George's Gallery, Hyde Park Corner. It is more than likely that these performers were from the Colony of Natal, to the south of the Zulu kingdom. Although the Zulu-speaking groups from this region had been excluded from the benefits of trade with the Portuguese at Delagoa Bay in present-day Mozambique by the first Zulu king, Shaka, they soon acquired large quantities of beads from the English traders who settled at Port Natal in the mid-1820s.*

Unfortunately, the details of dress and adornment recorded in Blackburn's watercolour are disappointingly sketchy. It is nevertheless clear from her image that the eleven men, one woman and a child who participated in these performances wore both beaded and leather garments. These items presumably were brought to London by the performers themselves, who were expected to create a suitably exotic impression to attract audiences keen to experience these and other spectacles of African 'savagery' at first hand. Since only two of these performers eventually returned to Natal, it is more than likely that their beadwork garments were ultimately acquired by curio collectors based in London.
Private collection, Cape Town

at the Msunduzi mission station, a considerable distance south-west of the border between the Colony and the kingdom.)[12]

Most of the beadwork pieces depicted in George Angas's folio volume, *The Kafirs illustrated* (1849), were also recorded among these Natal-based communities (see plate 10), mainly because the artist relied heavily on the assistance of the American missionaries who controlled some of the black locations on the outskirts of Durban. Although Angas did devote a few plates in his folio volume to illustrate beadwork from the Zulu kingdom (see plate 9) – viewed during his brief visit to the royal homestead of the third Zulu king, Mpande, in September 1847 – much of the available visual evidence regarding the early production of beadwork from the present-day KwaZulu-Natal region is restricted to the area under the Colony's control south of the Thukela river.[13]

The fact that outside visitors chose to collect beadwork pieces in this region in comparatively large quantities can also be ascribed, at least in part, to the emerging myth of the Zulu as a warrior nation, which was actively fostered both in the press and by London shows featuring Zulu-speaking men wearing full ceremonial military regalia (see plate 4).[14] This myth, which owes its origins to the early traders and missionaries who visited the first Zulu king, Shaka, and his immediate successor, Dingane (in the 1820s and 1830s),[15] was further reinforced by the 1849 publication of *The Kafirs illustrated,* which celebrated the exoticism of the Zulu-speaking communities Angas had encountered while travelling in the Colony of Natal and in the Zulu kingdom in the course of 1847. This was done in part through the inclusion of lengthy descriptions of the military prowess and supposed barbarism of the Zulu 'monarch' and his subjects.[16]

It seems reasonable to suggest that at least some of the beadwork pieces acquired in Britain over the past decade were bought in 19th-century London rather than the Colony of Natal. These pieces would have come either from the colonial agents responsible for mounting displays of 'native crafts' at successive 19th-century fairs and other commercially inspired ethnographic exhibitions aimed at capturing the imagination of British audiences keen to encounter, at first hand, the unfamiliar reality of 'primitive' or exotic cultures, or from Zulu-speaking performers participating in some of these London shows. Since many of these performers were ultimately abandoned by their agents, it is quite possible that they either sold or discarded their beadwork and other exotic costumes when thrown on their own resources. It is certainly remarkable that only two people out of the eleven men, one woman and a child who participated in an 1853 Zulu show eventually returned home,[17] while three Zulu-speaking women and a baby were abandoned by their London agent in December 1879.[18]

Other beadwork pieces no doubt were either looted or acquired as souvenirs by British soldiers who fought in the Anglo-Zulu war of 1879 and the South African War of 1899–1902. Although many of these – as well as a

5

Plate 5: This unusual photograph advertises the sale of curiosities like horns and karosses by the Durban-based firm, H.T. Peaches. Although no mention is made of beadwork in the advertising board included in the photograph, it is of course possible that the 'curiosities' available in the West Street area of central Durban may have included items of indigenous manufacture like the beaded items worn here by the Zulu dwarf, Jumbo. The heightened sense of otherness suggested by the presence in this image of a 35-year-old dwarf provides a very clear indication of the fact that early settlers and European visitors to the Colony of Natal viewed the indigenous communities they encountered as utterly distinct from themselves. This sense of difference, which obviously also extended to the wares these communities produced, is of considerable relevance to an understanding of the reasons early collectors acquired exotic curiosities like beadwork and other locally manufactured items.

Photograph: Michael Graham-Stewart collection

number of headrests and staffs – have ended up in regimental museums in Britain, the beaded items that have recently emerged from private homes suggest that many early visitors to South Africa relegated their souvenirs to long-forgotten attics and storerooms soon after they returned home.

The wealth of beadwork collected in present-day Kwazulu-Natal in the course of the 19th and early 20th centuries appears not to have been repeated elsewhere in the south-east African region. This is probably due largely to the fact that 'the Zulu' managed to capture the public's imagination in ways that were never matched by other southern African communities. Even in the Cape, where white settlers repeatedly confronted their Xhosa-speaking neighbours in a series of frontier wars, collecting practices do not seem to have been particularly widespread.[19] It would appear, in fact, that (if anything) souvenir collectors visiting the Cape in the course of the 19th century chose instead to acquire pieces produced by Zulu-speaking groups further afield.[20]

Even fewer late 19th- and early 20th-century beadwork pieces have emerged from communities to the north of the Zulu kingdom. This despite the fact that beads are known to have been used in *lobolo* (i.e. bridewealth) exchanges among various Tsonga-speaking groups,[21] many of whom produced heavy beaded belts and other beaded ornaments for use on festive occasions.[22] In view of the long history of Portuguese trading interests in present-day Mozambique, and the presence, also in this region, of Swiss missionaries in the late 19th and early 20th centuries, it is possible that some early beadwork pieces from the Delagoa Bay area may still emerge in Portugal or Switzerland.[23] But it seems unlikely that a search for early Tsonga pieces will ever yield a significant number of items from private Portuguese collections, in part because the traders who settled at Delagoa Bay probably had little if any interest in purchasing beadwork made from the beads they exchanged for valuable indigenous commodities like cattle, ivory and slaves. In contrast to this, there is considerable evidence to suggest that various Swiss missionaries expressed a keen interest in the arts produced by the Tsonga-speaking communities they encountered both in the Delagoa Bay region and in the northern Transvaal. But this interest appears to have been restricted almost entirely to the male domain of carving, notably headrests.[24]

With the exception of some pieces attributed to the Yao, very little of the material produced by communities further up the east coast and in the region of the eastern Zambezi has become available in recent years. Like most other groups from the south-east Africa region, the Yao once had easy access to east African traders, and are reputed to have exchanged slaves and ivory for beads and other trade goods in the course of the 19th century.[25] The often very large, densely woven beadwork fabrics produced by this group certainly provide clear evidence of the considerable wealth they succeeded in accumulating through this trade (see plates 6 and 7). But because of the lack of primary and even secondary material on this beadwork, very little seems to be known about these early Yao pieces.[26]

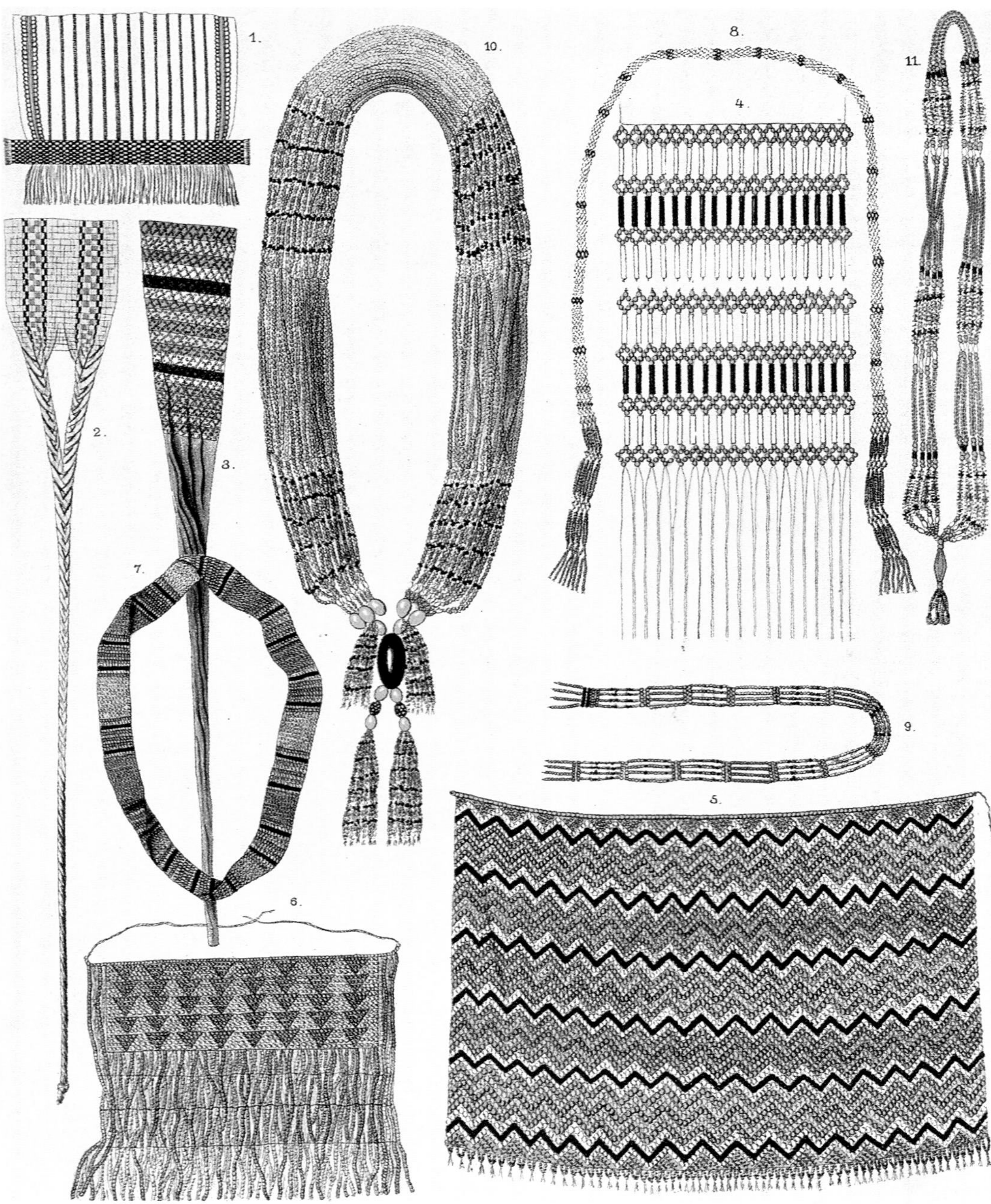

Plate 6: This plate is from H.P.N. Muller and J.F. Snelleman's c.1892 catalogue L'Industrie des Cafres du sud-est de l'Afrique, *which depicts a wide range of artefacts, including beaded objects and beadwork garments, from the south-east African region. According to the authors, by far the majority of the carved, woven and beaded artefacts they collected were from the Zambezi basin.*

L'Industrie des Cafres *is unusual not only because of the attention to details of craftmanship in the recording of individual objects, but also because the authors seldom ascribe precise ethnic designations to the works they collected. With the exception of no. 6, which they attributed to the 'Basoutos', the beadwork shown in this plate is simply labelled 'Zambese'. A skirt such as the one on the right is included in this book (no. 260).*

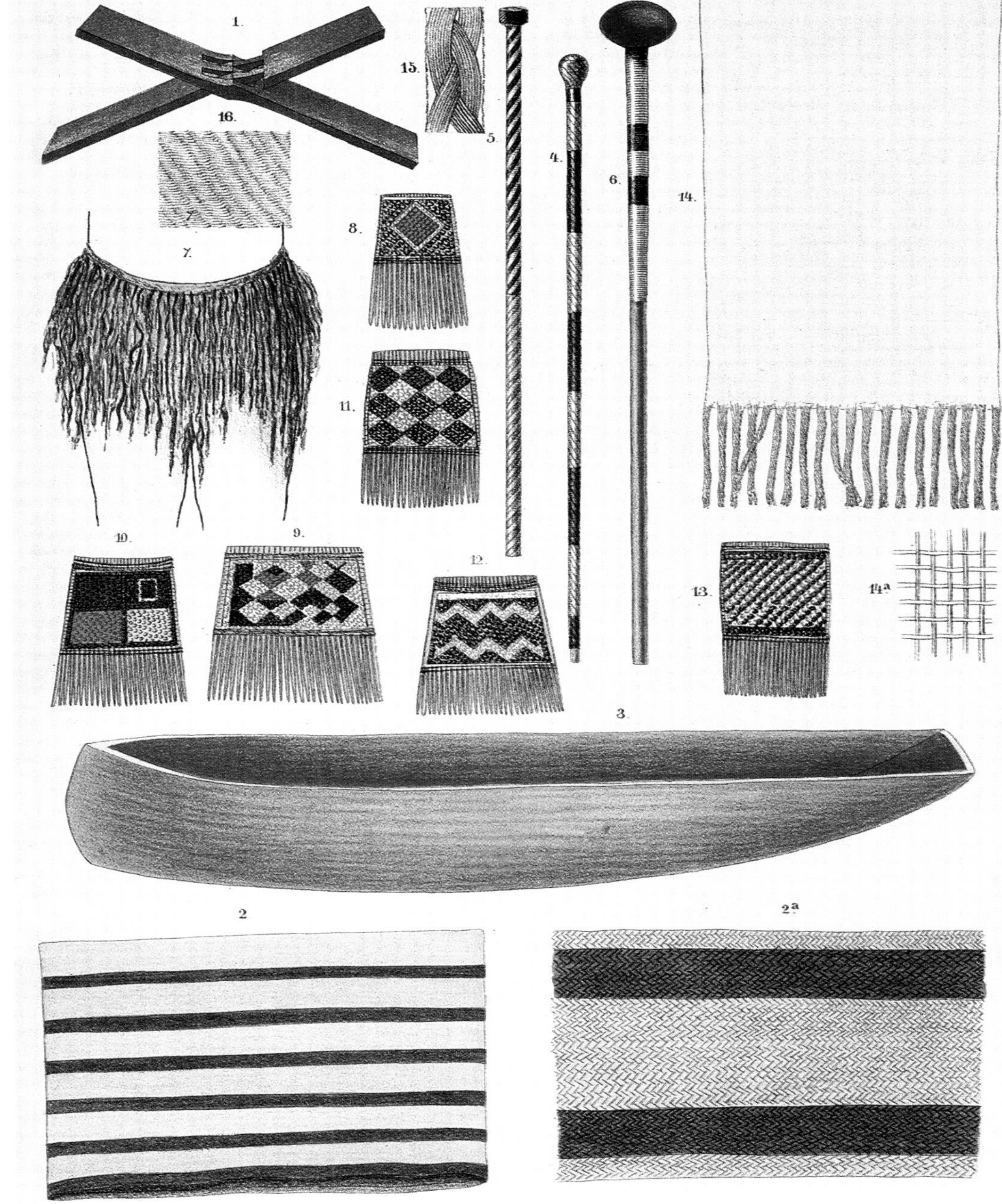

Plate 7: This plate from Muller and Snelleman's L'Industrie des Cafres du sud-est de l'Afrique *(c.1892) includes objects and artefacts from various areas in south-east Africa. The careful attention to detail in the beadwork found on the combs included in this plate – all of them labelled 'Zambese' – draws attention to the remarkable creativity of beadworkers, many of whom manipulated the aesthetic principles of symmetry that seem generally to inform the production of beadwork. Similar beaded combs are included in this book (nos. 252–259).*

8

Plate 8: This photograph depicts three pubescent girls wearing beadwork similar to that associated not only with the Pedi, but also with their Ntwane neighbours, most of whom settled at Kwarries-laagte in present-day Mpumalanga province in 1903, thereby ending a period of repeated migration during which they were influenced by a number of North Sotho groups. Because the hairstyles of these girls are consistent with those adopted to this day by young Ntwane initiates, the photograph was probably taken just before they entered the initiation lodge, or on their return from this period of seclusion, which is associated with instruction in the sexual and domestic roles women are expected to fulfill once they get married. Generally speaking, both the beadwork and the leather skirts worn by initiates belonging to groups that practise ceremonies of this kind are gender specific. This photograph does not, however, appear to have been taken with a view to highlighting the role ascribed to initiation practices by some Sotho- and Tsonga-speaking communities. It seems, instead, to have been set up in order to display various human and other 'native' specimens – like pots and baskets – for outside observers. The ethnographic function of photographs of this kind is further underlined by the fact that the three girls depicted in this image are framed by various natural props, among them the branch of a suitably exotic euphorbia tree.
Photograph: Michael Graham-Stewart collection

Beads v. indigenous materials

African communities with direct or indirect access to the Indian Ocean coastline began trading with Arab traders long before the arrival of European traders at Delagoa Bay and elsewhere, acquiring beads of Indian manufacture that are believed to have been produced as early as the 6th century BCE. These imported glass beads can be divided into three series: pale blue-green and yellow ones like those found at Mapungubwe and other sites in the Limpopo valley as early as the 10th century; more sophisticated beads of Indian manufacture that were traded successfully until the 19th century; and the beads of European origin that swamped the market thereafter.[27]

At Mapungubwe and similar major centres in the Limpopo valley, beads and other luxury goods appear to have formed part of a highly conspicuous pattern of consumption that witnessed the reworking of Indian beads into large, locally made ones, and that encouraged the emergence of similarly sophisticated artistic endeavours by metalsmiths, who produced animals and other prestige items from gold. At these centres, beadwork therefore played a very significant role in differentiating those in power from their subjects. People who lacked access to the benefits of trade continued to make ornaments from locally available seeds and grasses, in many cases in an effort to emulate the beadwork garments worn by indigenous elites, at least until the 1850s, when widespread access to imported glass beads became common throughout southern Africa.[28]

It is important to note, however, that items made from grass and other natural fibres were not necessarily replaced by beadwork pieces once the inhabitants of ordinary homesteads were able to acquire imported beads more readily. In some cases, like the grass belts that are still worn by married Zulu-speaking women, a detachable panel of beads was placed over the woven grasswork fabric, thus preserving the integrity of the original garment. The persistent use of grass in items of this kind can be ascribed to the fact that natural fibres seem to have played a significant role in expressing concerns involving notions of fertility. .To this day, therefore, grass is also used in the production of the costumes worn in various southern African communities by young post-pubescent girls during rites of passage that serve to celebrate their capacity to bear children. Perhaps most significantly, though, the importance ascribed to natural fibres is underlined by the crucial role they played in the annual First Fruits Ceremony, an important festival linked to the harvesting of the first summer crops during the reigns of Zulu king Shaka and his 19th-century successors. Highlighting the king's role in securing the fertility of the land and his people, this ceremony culminated in an early morning ritual at which the Zulu leader appeared dressed in a green costume made from newly harvested plant fibres.[29]

9

Plate 9: This plate, titled Two of King Panda's dancing girls, *is from George Angas's* The Kafirs illustrated *(1849). When Angas visited the Colony of Natal in 1847 he also spent a brief period at the royal homestead of the third Zulu king, Mpande, whose domain lay to the north-east of the newly established colony. Angas was clearly astonished by the large quantities of beadwork worn by members of the Zulu king's entourage, including the young women living in his royal enclosure. Referred to as the 'king's daughters', these young women in fact were 'given' to the Zulu leader by homestead heads across the kingdom, thereby allowing him to secure massive herds of cattle through bridewealth payments. The beadwork worn by these royal 'daughters' consisted of both large and small beads given to them by the king, who appears to have been responsible for choosing the colours they used in making their beaded garments.*

By the time Angas visited south-east Africa in the late 1840s, the techniques used in the production of beadwork had become comparatively sophisticated, probably because beads were more readily available (and therefore cheaper) than they had been earlier in the century. Although the older practice of wearing loose fronds of beadwork was not abandoned altogether, these new techniques involved the production of beadwork tapestries that were sewn together to form densely beaded fabrics over tubular ropes of grass.

Plate 10: Young Zulus in dancing costume *is one of the many images from Angas's* The Kafirs illustrated *recorded in one of the black locations established in the vicinity of Durban in the late 1840s. A number of these locations were controlled by American missionaries, several of whom provided the artist with accommodation. One of these American missionaries, Aldin Grout, travelled with Angas to the Zulu kingdom, where he met the third Zulu king, Mpande.*

According to Angas, the two young men depicted here, who were from Umlazi on the outskirts of Durban, were dressed for a 'marriage-dance'. In addition to the loose strands of beads still commonly worn at that time, the young man on the left wears a series of ropes of grass joined together intermittently with vertical strips of beadwork. Known as amabijo *(singular* umbijo*), in reference to the technique used to make beadwork items of this kind, these beaded ropes of grass (or, later, cloth) became increasingly popular after the mid-19th century. Although Angas's image of King Mpande's 'daughters' suggests that the practice of covering these ropes entirely with beads probably dates back to the early 1840s, it was only after beads became more readily available and inexpensive throughout the present-day KwaZulu-Natal region that tubular necklaces and waistbands produced in the* umbijo *technique began regularly to be covered entirely with beads.*

Although Angas annotated his original field sketches very carefully, these detailed notes were generally abandoned once he got back to his London studio, where formal considerations, like the need to balance the compositions of his lithographs, invariably won out. The beadwork colours found in his images are therefore not of much use in attempting to assess which bead colours may have been favoured in the various 'native' locations he visited during his stay in the Colony of Natal.

10

11

Plate 11: Mature women of rank attached to King Dingane's royal enclosure appear to have worn beadwork items and colours similar to those adopted by the king. These items were worn in conjunction with brass ornaments like neckrings and armbands that were fashioned at the king's court by royal metalsmiths. Like beads, this metal was obtained first through the Portuguese at Delagoa Bay, but later from English traders who settled at Port Natal in the 1820s. Both brass and beads generally were reserved for high-ranking officials. They therefore served to underline the status (and wealth) of the wearer. In the case of the king's female entourage, as can be seen in this print in Gardiner's Narrative of a journey to the Zoolu country *(1836), the status of older women (who were generally very highly regarded) was indicated further through the adoption of long leather skirts, though these appear to have been abandoned during the reign of King Mpande, who came to power in 1840.*

The changing fortune of beads

The symbolic significance ascribed to some indigenous materials notwithstanding, the value attached to beads changed radically in the course of the 19th century. Once the preserve of elite groups, they gradually assumed a host of new functions. Transformed into fashion items and used in courtship exchanges, their earlier importance in drawing attention to the status of chiefs and kings was irrevocably affected by the arrival in the area of large numbers of European traders.

In the eastern Cape, the exchange value of beads depreciated so markedly after the 1780s that they soon lost their importance in underlining differences in status and power.[30] At least until 1830, however, when this market became flooded with beads following a decision to lift a trade embargo between the Cape Colony and neighbouring Xhosa-speaking communities, Xhosa-speakers working for various missionaries were generally paid in beads.[31] During this period, moreover, the bead trade was so lucrative that some of these missionaries actually chose to abandon their commitment to the church, becoming traders instead.[32]

Further north, the relations between indigenous and settler communities were rather more complicated, in part because the numerous Zulu-speaking groups living beyond the borders of the Zulu kingdom had direct access to the European traders who settled at Port Natal in the mid-1820s. By the 1830s, the bead market in and around Port Natal had become so saturated that most of the local Zulu-speaking communities were increasingly unwilling to barter their fresh produce in exchange for beads. Writing in 1837, the Rev. Francis Owen, who arrived in Natal on his way to the Zulu kingdom, noted that his party had found great difficulty in getting 'a supply of our wants in this place, owing to the natives not choosing to accept the common articles of barter, which we had with us, beads and buttons. When we offered these in liberal quantities, they playfully threw dust into the air as a token of their contempt for these articles'.[33]

In the Zulu kingdom, further north, where a radically different situation prevailed – at least until the 1850s – the beads obtained first from the Portuguese at Delagoa Bay and later from the traders at Port Natal were delivered directly to the king, thereby ensuring royal control over their subsequent distribution. According to the Natal trader Nathaniel Isaacs, Shaka had an extreme aversion to 'anything like commercial traffic, and forbade it among his people'. He made it very clear to these traders that he would not be willing to tolerate any attempts to sell beads directly to his subjects.[34]

Throughout the reigns of Shaka and Dingane, visitors to the Zulu kingdom consequently found it difficult to exchange beads for food or other commodities when dealing with the heads of ordinary homesteads. As Smith observed in 1832: 'For the purchase of what the Zoolas have to dispose of, ... beads ... are of no avail, as no subject is either permitted to receive or possess them, unless as a gift from the king.'[35]

12

Plate 12: The Zulu king Dingane in his 'ordinary' and 'dance' dress, depicted by Gardiner in his Narrative of a journey to the Zoolu country *(1836). When the Rev. Francis Owen showed these images to Dingane in the late 1830s, the king remarked that they were poor likenesses, but was so impressed by the accuracy with which his beadwork garments had been recorded that he ordered one of the women in the royal enclosure to put them on for Owen's benefit. Generally speaking, the techniques used in the production of beaded items in the Zulu kingdom were still comparatively simple during the 1830s and 1840s. Several long strings of beads were often worn, bandolier-style, across the shoulders. Equally common was the practice of tying loose strings of beads together at one end before wrapping them around the head, neck, waist, arms or calves. The use of this comparatively simple technique made it difficult to introduce complex patterns through colour. In beadwork dating from this period, therefore, broad rectangular bands of colour tend to be juxtaposed to form stark colour contrasts. Unfortunately, the archeological evidence regarding the use of beadwork colours at Mgungundlovu, Dingane's royal homestead, is not particularly helpful in trying to determine which colours may have been favoured at that time.*

The contrast between the use of beads by these 'subjects' and the Zulu royal family was immediately and intentionally apparent. After Shaka's death in 1828, his personal property amounted to several tons of beads, brass and various other items.[36] This pattern of conspicuous consumption among the king and his immediate followers was to continue during the reigns of the second Zulu king, Dingane, and his successor, Mpande. Dingane was an enthusiastic promoter of several art forms, who always paid minute attention to details of costume and adornment,[37] while Mpande is known to have changed his beaded garments at least twice a day.[38]

When the Rev. Francis Owen visited Dingane's royal homestead, Mgungundlovu, in the late 1830s, the twenty-one posts supporting the large beehive structure where he entertained and received visitors were covered from top to bottom in beads of various colours.[39] The second Zulu king's obvious desire to display his wealth to foreign visitors was coupled with an abiding desire to know where these beads actually came from. Although rumour had it that they were from 'the bottom of the sea',[40] Dingane soon established that they were manufactured abroad and was therefore anxious to find out whether the art of making beads could in fact be taught to his own subjects.[41] Alternatively, he wanted to know whether it would be possible 'to get a bead-maker to live with him'.[42]

Dingane's evident pride in the beaded garments owned by him and by other members of his court is referred to repeatedly by missionaries like Gardiner, author of *Narrative of a journey to the Zoolu country* (1836),[43] and Champion, one of the first missionaries from the American Board of Commissioners to settle south of the Zulu kingdom in the course of the 1830s.[44] But his enthusiastic response to any mention of beads or beaded items is probably best illustrated by his reception of Gardiner's drawing of him wearing various beadwork garments (see plate 12). When these images of Dingane were first shown to him, the king 'could not be persuaded that the middle picture was at all like him. He mentioned someone else it resembled; but this did not dissuade him from immediately bringing out his beadwork to show the missionary their resemblance to [Gardiner's] drawings. He then had one of his women dressed out in them and got the long brass pole which he has in the picture ...'.[45]

More than ten years later little had changed. After the artist George Angas had visited King Mpande's royal homestead in 1847, he reported that 'On grand occasions the amount of beads worn by the king's women is almost incredible, a single dress having been known to consist of fifty pounds weight of these highly valued decorations, so as to render it a matter of some difficulty as well as personal inconvenience for the wearer to dance under the accumulated weight of her beads'.[46]

While the king's control over beadwork depreciated noticeably over the following few years when Mpande found it increasingly difficult to monitor the interactions between his subjects and the growing number of Natal

Plate 13: Studio photograph of a married woman by J.E. Middlebrook probably dating from the 1880s. These studio photographs of Zulu-speakers from the Colony of Natal, south of the Zulu kingdom, became increasingly popular as postcards and tourist mementos in the second half of the 19th century. Like Angas's lithographs for The Kafirs illustrated *(1849), most of them depict people living in the black locations established in the Durban area in the late 1840s.*

Although there is evidence to suggest that pre-pubescent girls and boys from the present-day KwaZulu-Natal region wore necklaces that differed in style from those worn by adults, none of the 19th-century beaded necklaces used by these adult men and women appear to have had a gender-specific function. In contrast to men, however, married women generally wore a thin strip of beadwork across their foreheads as a sign of respect to their husbands and parents-in-law. Known as an umnqwazi, *this beaded ornament was originally made from grass.*

Photograph: Michael Graham-Stewart collection

traders streaming into the kingdom, beads nevertheless remained a highly valued commodity for some time thereafter. Catherine Barter, who travelled to the Zulu kingdom in 1855, noted, for example, that a calf could still be bought there for a cotton blanket, while a more substantial blanket and a couple of strings of large red beads could purchase 'very fine cattle'.[47] Until the destruction of the Zulu kingdom in 1879 it was therefore the more affluent homesteads, with sufficient cattle to exchange for large quantities of luxury goods like beads, that tended to engage in barter of this kind.

Fashion v. the symbolic use of colour

Unfortunately, our understanding of the possible symbolic significance of 19th-century bead colours and styles is severely hampered by a lack of adequate oral evidence on the comparative importance of factors like individual creativity, the dictates of fashion, and the need to communicate social and/or religious values. Mainly for these reasons, the available literature often seems confusing and even contradictory. These issues of interpretation are further complicated by the fact that beads obtained from older beadwork pieces were sometimes re-used in new pieces for reasons of both economy and symbolism. This makes it extremely difficult not only to date particular beadwork items with any degree of certainty, but also to access the meanings that may have been ascribed to them.

Although, in the Zulu kingdom, beads were used mainly to articulate hierarchical relations of power, considerable symbolic importance was attached to the use of specific colours, notably red. When Smith visited the kingdom in 1832, he mentioned that Dingane wanted 'blood red and rose coloured [beads], but in the absence of such would accept white tembos, when not too small and also the dark blue'.[48] Some years later, the philologist, Bleek, noted that a woman from King Mpande's royal court had dreamt that he 'would give her small red beads'.[49]

It will probably never be entirely clear why red beads were favoured in the Zulu kingdom throughout the 19th century. It may, however, be relevant to a consideration of the Zulu interest in these beads that a survey of the beadwork produced by Xhosa-speaking groups from the area to the south of the Zulu kingdom suggests that the preference some Xhosa groups showed for red beads can be linked to the use of red ochre. According to the authors of this survey, 'red appears to have been the colour of cosmetics which denoted a stable and normal state....'[50] They also note that, among these Xhosa-speaking groups, red beads were and still are used in contexts of chieftainship.

In the Zulu kingdom, red ochre had a similarly important function. It was used to dress the tufts of hair or top-knots on the heads of married women, and it continues to be used in divination contexts to this day.[51] For the obvious reason that it is the colour of (menstrual) blood, contemporary Zulu-speakers often associate red with fertility.[52] Although

14

Plate 14: A studio photograph of a young man wearing a beaded necklace almost identical in design to the married woman's necklace recorded by Middlebrook (plate 13), and with a pattern similar to its zigzag motif. However, judging from the comparatively few light or white beads included in the necklace worn by this young man, it must have differed considerably in appearance from the necklace worn by the married woman in Middlebrook's photograph.

A number of different techniques were used in making these necklaces. Long, rectangular beadwork tapestries, which were commonly known as amageko *(singular* umgeko*), usually were tied around the neck either with delicately beaded strings, as in Middlebrook's photograph, or with thick beadwork ropes, as in this image. Small rectangular pieces worn across the forehead and beaded earrings were also quite common.*
Photograph: Cape Archives

there is no irrefutable evidence to suggest that this colour symbolism necessarily underlay the royal interest in red beads in the Zulu kingdom, it is probably not coincidental that these beads were known as *umgazi*, i.e. blood. The latter designation is especially interesting given that considerable attention was paid to the potentially powerful role of material symbols in reinforcing a perception of the king's importance in fertility rites like the annual First Fruits Ceremony.

Unfortunately, however, attempts to reconstruct the possible symbolic implications of beadwork colours (and patterns) are limited by the fact that early visitors to the kingdom seem not to have been interested in the possibility that choices of this kind may have been made to communicate visually some or other aspect of the social or religious values of a community. The evidence afforded by other sources, notably the oral histories collected by James Stuart[53] among Zulu-speakers in the late 19th and early 20th centuries, although more promising, is also quite problematic, mainly because these oral histories are often surprisingly contradictory. While this confusion may be due in part to the fact that Stuart himself had little interest in recording information on the material culture of the Zulu-speakers he interviewed, it is important to note that 19th-century travellers and traders repeatedly drew attention to the interest communities expressed in acquiring fashionably new or unusual bead colours. Thus, for example, when Ludlow visited the Zulu kingdom immediately after it was defeated by the British in 1879, he recorded that 'In one district black and white beads were much sought after. Girls crowded around our huts for them, and many came from long distances to get the precious beads. At another kraal, green and pink were in high favour, and they would not look at the black and white ones, while some beads not of the latest shade in pink they would not accept. Those which seemed most to take their fancy – large red ones worn around the neck – before the war were reserved for Cetshwayo's wives and daughters'.[54]

It seems safe to conclude not only that some beadwork styles were probably quite short-lived, but also that many of them do not necessarily attest to the overt expression of any particular symbolic concern. This is confirmed by Bishop Colenso who wrote on his first visit to the Colony of Natal in 1854 that '[t]he Natives... are as capricious in their taste for beads, as any English lady in the choice of her bonnet. The same pattern will only suit them for a season or two; and they are at all times difficult to please'.[55]

15

Plate 15: Studio photograph of a young Zulu-speaking man from southern Natal wearing an exceptionally rich array of beadwork in a variety of patterns and colours, including beaded earrings and a beaded collar similar to that worn by both men and women in the late 19th and early 20th centuries. The adoption, during this period, of ropes and belts as armbands (and even as necklaces) is consistent with the growing practice in late 19th-century Natal of creating a strong visual impression by combining densely woven beadwork fabrics with a variety of items obtained from the increasing number of 'native' stores established on the black locations in the Durban area.

The extravagant hairstyles adopted by these young men from the southern Natal region encouraged a number of white observers to describe them as 'Zulu dandies'. But people living in the Zulu kingdom generally referred to them, derogatorily, as iziyendane, *i.e. those with strange hairstyles. It is not clear where or when these hairstyles arose but, like the beadwork worn by many of these southern Natal 'dandies', their hair seems to have played a role in their apparent refusal to conform to the new 'European' dress codes that were then being imposed on the members of indigenous communities seeking to enter white urban areas.*

See nos. 214–216 for beadwork similar to the sash the young man is wearing across his shoulder.
Imprinted: 'Published by Sallo Epstein & Co., Durban.'
Photograph: Michael Graham-Stewart collection

Looking for meaning in style: ethnicity v. regionalism

Despite the evidence pointing to the role fashion played in the acquisition of particular beadwork colours, it has always been assumed that most beadwork styles give expression to some or other aspect of group identity. While this is undoubtedly relevant to a consideration of developments in the early 20th century, when successive white governments relied on ethnic designations to allocate land to South Africa's black communities, it is also possible that similarly pragmatic concerns may have contributed to, and sometimes even dictated, the development of particular beadwork styles earlier on. In other words, notions of ethnic or group identity were not simply imposed from above by 20th-century white ideologues. On the contrary, as Hamilton has noted, 'Apartheid policies were effective precisely because they were not complete inventions, but sophisticated reworkings of already extant ideas, in the service of domination'.[56]

The importance of this assertion notwithstanding, it is often quite difficult to reconstruct the relationship between the precolonial and colonial identities of communities living in the south-east African region. In the case of beadwork, this is due partly to the absence of any clear provenance for almost all 19th-century beadwork pieces. But it can also be ascribed to a number of socio-cultural and political factors.

In some areas, struggles to effect control over resources like land and imported materials often encouraged loosely organised kinship groups to form larger alliances. This can certainly be said of communities to the south of the Zulu kingdom, where numerous Zulu-speaking groups had a long history of opposition to Shaka and his successors. Forced into tributary relations by successive Zulu kings, these groups developed very distinctive styles of dress and personal adornment, at least in part in an attempt to highlight their sense of difference from their Zulu-speaking neighbours to the north.

But such evidence pointing to the emergence of 'ethnic' styles has had an arguably negative impact on the scholarly endeavours of South African beadwork specialists, several of whom have devoted enormous resources to studying the possible connections between specific group identities – both in the 19th and 20th centuries – and particular beadwork patterns and colours. This trend, which is reflected most recently in many of the essays included in *Evocations of the child. Fertility figures from the southern African region*,[57] certainly can and often does provide fascinating insights both into relations between various 19th-century communities, and the ways in which formerly fluid and often hybrid identities were manipulated by the state in the course of the 20th century. But it does not necessarily follow from the evidence afforded by, for example, the attempts of communities like the Ndebele to affirm a sense of group identity in the hope of securing land, or the opposition of some Zulu-speaking groups to Shaka and his successors, that the patterns and colours found

16

Plate 16: Young girl, probably from southern Natal, wearing a number of beaded necklaces and waistbands made in a variety of different ways. In addition to one necklace made from unusually large beads, she has a rope-like necklace with beads wound around it in a diagonal or spiral formation, another (made from two contrasting colours) in which a somewhat different technique has been used, and, below that, two necklaces made from individual strings of beads twisted around one another to form loose but thick rope-like strands. As this indicates, variations in design were sometimes introduced through the use of different techniques rather than particular beadwork patterns and colours.
Photograph: National Library of S.A., Cape Town

in all 19th-century beadwork pieces are necessarily ethnically coded.

At least, in some areas, the need actively to assert a common identity prior to the arrival of white settlers appears not to have been particularly pressing. Thus, for example, according to Harries, the emergence in the late 19th century of a Tsonga identity among various groups living in present-day Mozambique can be attributed largely to missionary concerns to standardise and codify linguistic forms for biblical instruction.[58] Here, and elsewhere, researchers have consequently highlighted the evidence pointing to the presence of regional rather than ethnic styles for headrests and other artefacts.[59]

Since in many cases 19th-century settlement patterns did not necessarily coincide with the 'clans' or larger group identities generally invoked by researchers seeking to ascribe ethnic labels to particular beadwork styles,[60] this evidence pointing to the presence of regional styles is hardly surprising. Throughout the southern African region, most people actually lived in agnatic clusters rather than 'clans', and even when these clusters formed part of larger chiefdoms or polities, the social and cultural boundaries between different communities were not necessarily carefully defined. A very clear indication that interactions between different groupings were (and are) often fluid and open-ended is provided by Henri-Phillipe Junod's observation that the beadwork produced by Tsonga-speakers who had moved from present-day Mozambique to the Transvaal in the course of the 19th century attested to the influence of neighbouring Ndebele communities by the 1930s.[61] It has been argued, likewise, that the Ntwane, who now live in Mpumalanga province, adopted dress codes and other styles similar to those of their Pedi neighbours after they settled at Kwarrieslaagte in 1903.[62]

The creative role of women

One of the most under-explored issues regarding the spread and possible meaning of beadwork styles concerns the physical mobility of newly married women. Like their 20th-century successors, most 19th-century women learnt the art of beadwork from their mothers and grandmothers. But while the majority probably remained close to their agnatic homes after marriage, often moving little more than a few kilometres from their parents' homesteads, some definitely ended up in areas further afield. As this suggests, the spread of beadwork styles generally would have been quite unpredictable, in some cases leading to the adoption of certain motifs and colours in a number of different places at any particular time. There is also considerable evidence to suggest that creative interactions between incoming and already established beadmakers probably encouraged the development of hybrid bead styles in some areas.

Other factors that may have influenced women either to repeat already established styles and techniques, or to produce innovative work, must also be acknowledged. Thus, although some beadwork styles undoubtedly provide indisputable evidence of a willingness to (re)affirm a sense of

17

*Plate 17: An unusual photograph depicting an unmarried woman flanked by two married women with top-knots, one of them wearing the leather skirt (*isidwaba*) adopted by Zulu-speaking women after their bridewealth had been paid in full. Taken near Volksrust in the south-western Transvaal, the exceptionally rich array of beadwork worn by these women includes a large number of necklaces, beaded waistbands and other beadwork panels. In addition to this, they all have strings of beadwork wound around their elbows, wrists and ankles, as well as brass-wire leg- and armbands, known as* amasongo.

The style of the beadwork worn by these women is very similar to that recorded in the late 19th century among members of the Hlubi, a group that originated in the Lubombo mountains near Swaziland, but was forced to migrate several times in the course of the 19th century before settling in the Drakensberg region. This apparent visual evidence notwithstanding, it is highly unlikely that the beadwork depicted here might point to a connection either with the Hlubi or with their ancestors in the south-western Transvaal. This lack of certainty can be ascribed partly to the fact that most southern African chiefdoms were made up of a fluctuating number of local communities prior to the intervention in indigenous political structures of white colonial officials. Like the Hlubi oral historian who claimed that 'we are one with the Swazis as well as the Basutos', many therefore tended to emphasise complex historical relations to other communities in the region. But even when communities remained stable over a long period, they did not necessarily feel the need to give expression – through material symbols like beadwork and other forms of dress and adornment – to a sense of group cohesion. Instead, women often borrowed styles and motifs to create vibrant, hybrid forms that served, above all, to underline their own fashionableness.

Inscribed on reverse: 'Photo by Rev. L. Trevor Sadler, Volksrust, Transvaal [1914]'. Published in *The foreign field*, February 1923.

Photograph: Michael Graham-Stewart collection

group identity, it would be nothing short of absurd to suggest that all stylistic decisions were (or are) necessarily informed by a desire to reflect socio-political identities. This point has been made very clearly by Davison[63] who notes that it is more than likely that aesthetic choices would have been shaped, not only by cultural and historical factors, but also by more subjective concerns. The decision to add manufactured European buckles to the early beaded belts collected among various Zulu-speaking groups is an obvious case in point. Because the role of recycled items of this kind appears to have been quite sporadic, they clearly underline the role of individual taste or choice on the part of the makers and/or users of beadwork. It is equally possible that many other design features ultimately attest to the innovation and creativity of individual beadmakers. Thus, for example, while it has become common practice to attach ethnic labels to beadwork items that include mother-of-pearl buttons,[64] the interest Mfengu and other women from the eastern Cape expressed in this trade item presumably was stimulated in the first instance by the shimmering visual effects that could be achieved by placing several of them alongside one another.

On the other hand, there is also evidence to suggest that, at least in the Zulu kingdom, women were not necessarily responsible for making important decisions regarding bead-work colours and styles. Instead, these styles generally were dictated by rigidly enforced rules aimed at underlining hierarchically structured social relations. This is amply demonstrated by the fact that, at the annual First Fruits Ceremony during Dingane's reign, some of the girls from the king's royal enclosure wore 'only white beads, others only blue, others another colour'.[65] According to Paulina Dlamini, who was attached to King Cetshwayo's royal homestead, Ondini, in the 1870s, these *umdlunkulu* girls, all of whom belonged to particular 'regiments', continued to wear bead colours (and cloths) chosen for them by the king even after the trade between Natal and the kingdom had eroded the king's control over beads.[66]

Whether successive 19th-century Zulu kings also controlled other aspects of beadwork design remains unclear. It seems more than likely, however, that many changes, including technical modifications, would have been introduced in response not so much to royal decree as to both the growing availability of beads and the development of new techniques among groups to the south of the Thukela river, where the creative skills of women were not constrained by royal regulations. Either way, the beadwork items worn both by the king and by the women from the *isigoldo* or royal enclosure were comparatively simple during Dingane's reign. In contrast to the densely woven beaded fabrics commonly worn after the mid-19th century, these garments usually consisted of beads strung into loose vertical fronds joined at the top by a single horizontal thread. Judging from drawings in Gardiner's *Narrative of a journey to the Zoolu country* (see plates 11 and 12), as well as later examples from Angas's *The Kafirs illustrated* (see plates 9 and 10), these fronds were usually arranged to form broad horizontal bands of colour that

18

Plate 18: This photograph was reproduced in A.T. Bryant's Olden times in Zululand and Natal *(1928). Titled 'Two young youths go out a-courting', it is remarkable for depicting two unusually self-assured young men wearing a large number of beadwork pieces on their heads and around their necks, waists and legs. Since the beadwork worn by young Zulu men was generally given to them by female admirers, they effectively advertised their popularity for all to see by covering themselves in beaded ornaments. There is evidence to suggest that, at least in some south-east African communities, male fears of being ridiculed as sexually unattractive were so great that young men often prevailed upon their female relatives to make beadwork pieces for them to wear on festive occasions.*

were worn on the side of the head, around the neck, and on the upper arm and calf.

In the course of the 1840s, these loose fronds slowly gave way either to densely woven beadwork fabrics, or to the use of tubular ropes of cloth or grass around which beads were strung in spiral-like formations. In the latter case, up to half of the beads would no longer have been visible. At least initially, economy in the use of beads in pieces of this kind was achieved by leaving sections of the grass or cloth exposed, but it soon became increasingly common to cover these tubes entirely with beads.

Even in the Zulu kingdom, therefore, it is likely that certain innovations and transformations were predicated on the growing availability of beads by the mid-19th century. It was, in fact, above all because of this availability that women throughout southern Africa were afforded the opportunity to develop their creative skills in the second half of the 19th century, leading to an extraordinary flowering of beadwork production throughout the region. No longer a valuable item of exchange, beadwork nevertheless remained a significant symbolic commodity that continues to this day to play a role in the articulation of social relations among rural traditionalists.

The role of beadwork in the articulation of male and female spheres of power and influence

In some south-east African areas, beadwork played a very significant role both in courtship relations and in dowry payments. In the Colony of Natal, for example, brides generally took large quantities of beadwork with them to their future husbands' homes. Prior to getting married, these young women also made beadwork pieces for their potential or future husbands as an expression of affection or appreciation, a practice that has encouraged a host of popular – and academic – writers to explore the possible meanings of bead colours in so-called 'love letter' necklaces from the present-day KwaZulu-Natal region.[67]

There was an equally significant relationship between beads, courtship and dowry payments in the eastern Cape, where much of the beadwork made by young women was given to men.[68] In the early 19th century when beads were still a valuable economic commodity, the exchange value of the bride wealth, i.e. cattle, men paid for their future wives was probably more or less equivalent to that of the beadwork items brides (and their families) gave to their future husbands prior to their weddings.[69]

In the past, researchers generally assumed that dowries and dowry-like payments of this kind probably gave women greater economic security, status and independence, but this

19

Plate 19: A photograph of Chief Mangosuthu Buthelezi, South Africa's present Minister of Home Affairs, taken at his inauguration in 1958 as chief of the Buthelezi. A royal Zulu group, the Buthelezi are related to, and have maintained very close links with, the Zulu royal family at least since the reign of King Cetshwayo, who was deposed by British forces in 1879.

Like the members of almost all indigenous elites, the Zulu royal family abandoned the practice of wearing beadwork and other traditional forms of dress in the early 20th century, mainly due to pressure from white missionaries seeking to 'civilise' rural African communities. It was only in 1954, when a decision was made to unveil a memorial to the first Zulu king, Shaka, that Buthelezi and his cousin, King Cyprian, decided to attend part of this ceremony in newly made and borrowed skins and beadwork. Their seemingly sudden decision to wear 'traditional' dress on this occasion owed much to the emergence of African liberation movements throughout the continent in the 1940s. Tired of being treated as inferior, these African intellectuals sought to affirm and validate indigenous cultural practices. In keeping with this trend, the well-known Zulu author H.I.E. Dhlomo wrote an essay entitled 'The Zulu and his beads' in which he claimed a spiritual, even mystical significance for beadwork.

Despite these attempts to rehabilitate the art of beadwork in the eyes of educated Africans, Zulu-speaking Christians ridiculed Buthelezi for wearing beaded and other traditional items when he took office as chief of the Buthelezi in 1958. On that occasion, his dress included a very rare leopard tooth necklace interspersed with large red beads. This heirloom, which once belonged to a member of the Zulu royal family, was probably saved from destruction because of the enormous symbolic importance 19th-century leaders ascribed to both leopard skin and large red beads as symbols of power and authority.
Photograph: S.P. Bourquin

view has recently been challenged by evidence suggesting that dowries effectively reinforce the inequality in women's and men's relationship to property by cancelling women's right to land and other assets following the death of their fathers.[70] Judging from the beadwork Xhosa-speaking women made for their lovers and future husbands, these inequalities often extended beyond the material realm, for gifts of this kind also played an important role in perpetuating the male domain, ultimately reinforcing the significance of a symbolic order dominated by the experiences of men rather than women. In other words, beadwork dowries generally served to confirm existing social relations and divisions between Xhosa-speaking men and their wives. This does not, however, mean that female beadworkers were little more than passive reflectors of a world centred around their lovers and husbands. On the contrary, as the producers of the beadwork that men wore, women obviously played a significant role in constructing and even transforming that world, constantly manipulating both the symbolic and aesthetic canons they had inherited from their mothers and grandmothers.

Revisiting the past: proud owners of beadwork in the late 20th century

In a photograph taken at the Mariannhill Mission Station in the late 19th century (plate 18), two young men display their rich collection of beadwork with obvious pride. Clearly confident in the face of the camera, they are dressed as though in preparation for attending an important social event like a wedding, or to court perhaps the young women from whom they received some of their beaded items.[71] In an era that witnessed the triumph of missionary activities, leading to the demand that African communities adopt the dress of their European masters, the self-assurance displayed by these young men seems nothing short of remarkable. It was not until the early 20th century, however, that the relentless attack on traditionalist values and practices began to have a demonstrable impact on the lives of those who sought to hold on to the beliefs and dress codes of their ancestors. Commenting on his memories of life at the Zulu royal court in the 1930s, Chief Mangosuthu Buthelezi, South Africa's present Minister of Home Affairs (see plate 19), noted that, 'When I was a child I remember that my cousins the Zulu Princesses at the Royal Palace of my uncle King Solomon kaDinuzulu where I grew up, were often chided by their teachers and the priest's wife if they adorned themselves with beadwork. It was just not done. It was "unChristian". It was not a thing for Christian girls to wear what was regarded as gear worn only by so-called Heathens.'[72]

According to Buthelezi, attitudes like these continued to inform the perceptions of Christian Zulu-speakers as late as the 1950s: 'I recall that when... the Buthelezi... wanted to hold the traditional ceremony to install me as their traditional hereditary leader, there were reactions in my Anglican parish, when I was dressed up in traditional dress for the occasion by my family and the councillors. A prominent

20

Plate 20: South Africa's first black president, Nelson Mandela, photographed shortly after the African National Congress was voted into office in April 1994. During the lead-up to this historic democratic election, Mandela was repeatedly offered gifts of beadwork by rural traditionalists. As a royal descendant of one of the Xhosa-speaking groups from the eastern Cape, he graciously accepted the Thembu tobacco bags, blankets and beadwork given to him on these occasions. But he himself seems never to have chosen to wear beaded garments of any kind since his release from prison in 1990. This is most probably due to the fact that Mandela has repeatedly affirmed the need to overcome ethnic divisions in post-apartheid South Africa, which are often clearly articulated in 20th-century beadwork styles. In one now famous quotation, he is reported to have said: 'I respect custom, but I am not a tribalist.'

Despite this recent desire actively to avoid any accusations of favouring Thembu (or Xhosa) tradition, it is interesting to note that Mandela deliberately wore beaded garments when he was sentenced to life imprisonment in the early 1960s. The motivation behind this powerful symbolic statement became very clear in Mandela's speech from the dock in which he questioned the legitimacy of his standing accused in a white man's court by a white prosecutor under white man's laws before a white judge. At the time of Mandela's trial, many of the people who attended the court proceedings voiced their protest against the apartheid regime in the same way, by wearing beadwork and other 'traditional' ornaments and garments. In keeping with developments of this kind, the Congress-aligned newspaper, New Age, *published an article in 1962 in which it posed the question: 'Should African leaders wear tribal dress?' This piece included a number of interesting responses by ANC leaders and supporters, among them President Mandela's former wife Winnie, who responded by saying: 'We are Africans and need not regret that we were born Africans.'*

Photograph: Guy Tillim

lady who worshipped with me... suggested that I should be excommunicated'.[73]

This erosion of traditionalist practices has since been reversed partly through the efforts of organisations like the Congress of Traditional Leaders of South Africa, founded in 1987,[74] and the revival in the course of the 1980s and 1990s of rituals and dress codes that were abandoned in the early 20th century.[75] Several reasons may be cited for this renewed interest in beadwork and other traditional forms of dress and adornment.

Already in the late 1970s, in the aftermath of the Soweto Uprising of 1976 and the emergence thereafter of the Black Consciousness Movement, various student and other leaders called for a rejection of Western forms of dress. Similar statements of protest against South Africa's white minority government continued throughout the 1980s, but it was only after the unbanning of various political organisations in 1990, and the assumption of power by the African National Congress in 1994, that the country's new black elite began actively to embrace indigenous forms of dress and to adorn themselves with beadwork items similar to those worn by rural traditionalists.

Throughout South Africa, beadworkers have begun to cater for this new market, producing work aimed at capturing the eye of fashion-conscious individuals seeking to express a sense of pride in the cultural heritage of their ancestors.[76] In most cases, the beaded necklaces and armbands produced for this market have little if anything in common with the work beadmakers produce for rural traditionalists, partly because unusual metallic colours are used in the making of these fashionable beadwork pieces. More traditional pieces are assuming a somewhat different role in the lives of patriotic South Africans anxious to reclaim their past. Framed behind glass and displayed on the walls of countless politicians and business executives, these items of adornment have finally been transformed into works of art. It is therefore not only in the context of the gallery, but now also in the private homes of many of the descendants of the 19th-century beadworkers who made these pieces, that beadwork items have assumed a meaning that would have been unimaginable to their original producers and owners.

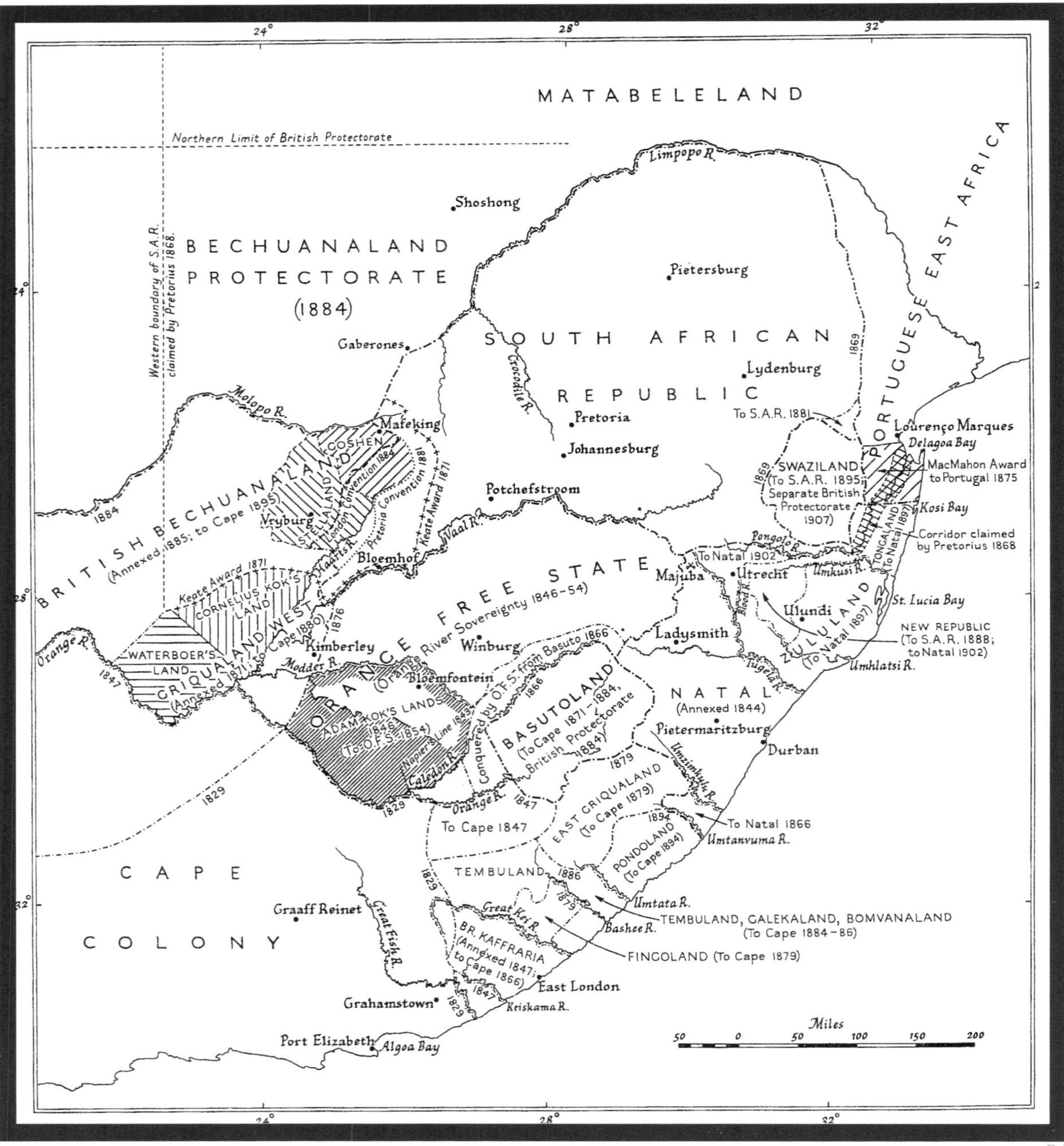

Plate 21:
Frontier changes in south-east Africa in the 19th century
From An atlas of African history *by J.D. Fage*
Printed in Great Britain in 1958

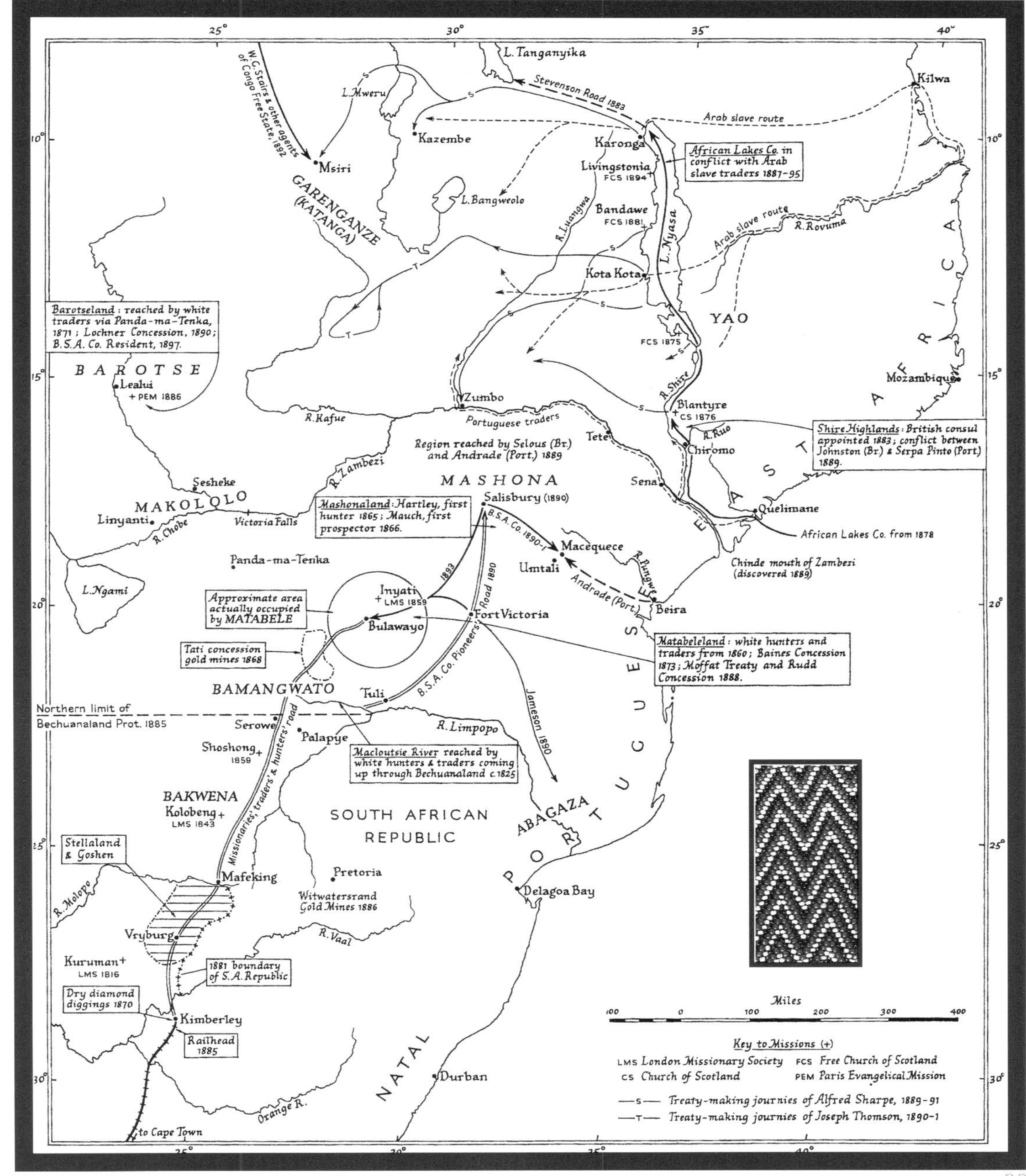

Plate 22:
Expansion of European trade and Christian missions in central and south-east Africa
From An atlas of African history *by J.D. Fage*
Printed in Great Britain in 1958

SOUTH-EAST AFRICAN BEADWORK 1850–1910

right:
1. South Nguni
Beaded breast-cover
mid 19th century
69 x 37cm

cf. M. Carey, *Beads and beadwork of East and South Africa*, 1986, p. 33; and E.M. Shaw and N.J. van Warmelo, 'Material culture of the Cape Nguni', *Annals of the S.A. Museum*, vol. 58(4), p. 535, pl. 80(6), and p. 605, pl. 96(2).
See pl. no. 1 for late 19th-century photograph of women wearing similar breast-covers.

Use of terms

Specific group identities have been ascribed to individual beadwork items where these are known. In most cases, however, it is neither possible, nor is it appropriate, to resort to designations of this kind. Most of the beadwork pieces listed in the catalogue have therefore simply been labelled 'North Nguni' or 'South Nguni' and, in a few cases, 'Drakensberg region'. 'Nguni' is the generic term adopted by academics in the 1930s to describe the communities that historically had inhabited the region from Swaziland to the eastern Cape. In keeping with this classificatory system, 'North Nguni' is used here to refer to groups residing in Swaziland, the Zulu kingdom, and the Colony of Natal, while the term 'South Nguni' encompasses the Xhosa-speaking groups that settled further south. The designation 'Drakensberg region' has been adopted for some beadwork pieces in the interest of avoiding a false sense of certainty regarding interactions between the various communities that either settled permanently, or moved in and out of this region during the course of the 19th century.

The description of each piece is limited to form and function, where known. Because many pieces could have been worn by either a man or a woman, references to gender have in almost all instances been avoided.

The term 'late 19th century' is used to cover the period circa 1880–1910.

The dimensions of each piece are approximate because of their often irregular size. Height is given before width in all instances except waist-bands and belts where length is given before width.

1

detail, no. 3

left:
detail, no. 3

right:
2. South Nguni
Beaded cloth bag
mid to late 19th century
bag: 20 x 16cm

cf. *Art and ambiguity*, Johannesburg, 1991, fig.102, p.118.

3. South Nguni
Beaded cloth bag
mid 19th century
bag: 27 x 17cm

following two pages:
left:
4. South Nguni, Mfengu
Beaded cloth bag
early 20th century
bag: 22.5 x 16cm

5. South Nguni, probably Thembu
Beaded cloth bag
late 19th century
bag: 22.5 x 14cm

right:
6. South Nguni, Mfengu
Beaded cloth bag
early 20th century
bag: 22.5 x 16cm

7. South Nguni, Mfengu
Beaded cloth bag
early 20th century
bag: 22 x 17cm

2

3

4

5

6

7

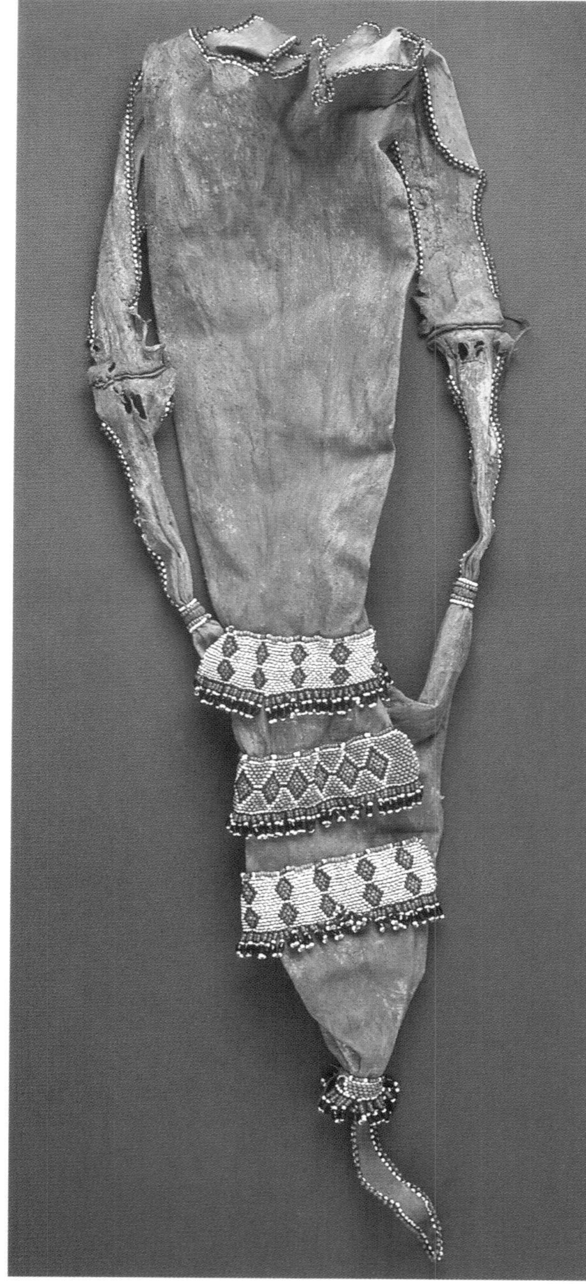

8

9

left:

8. South Nguni, Mfengu
Beaded goatskin tobacco bag
late 19th century
length: 90cm (approximately)

9. South Nguni, Mfengu
Beaded leather bag
late 19th century
bag: 32.5 x 21cm

Provenance for the above two bags:
Alfred John Gregory (1851–1927), who lived at the Cape between 1891 and 1914 and served as Medical Officer of Health for the Cape Colony between 1901 and 1910.
See DSAB, vol. 5.

right:

10. Southern Drakensberg region
Beaded leather waistband with apron
second half 19th century
60 x 23cm

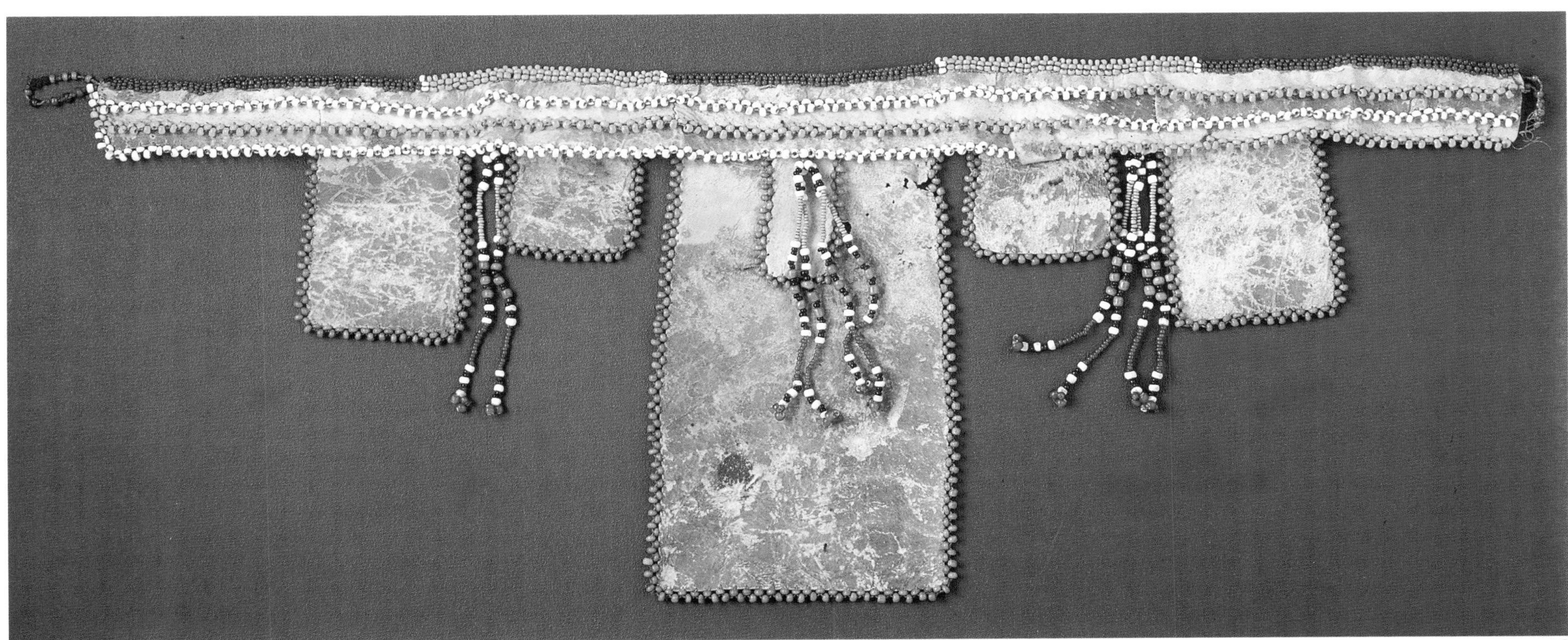

10

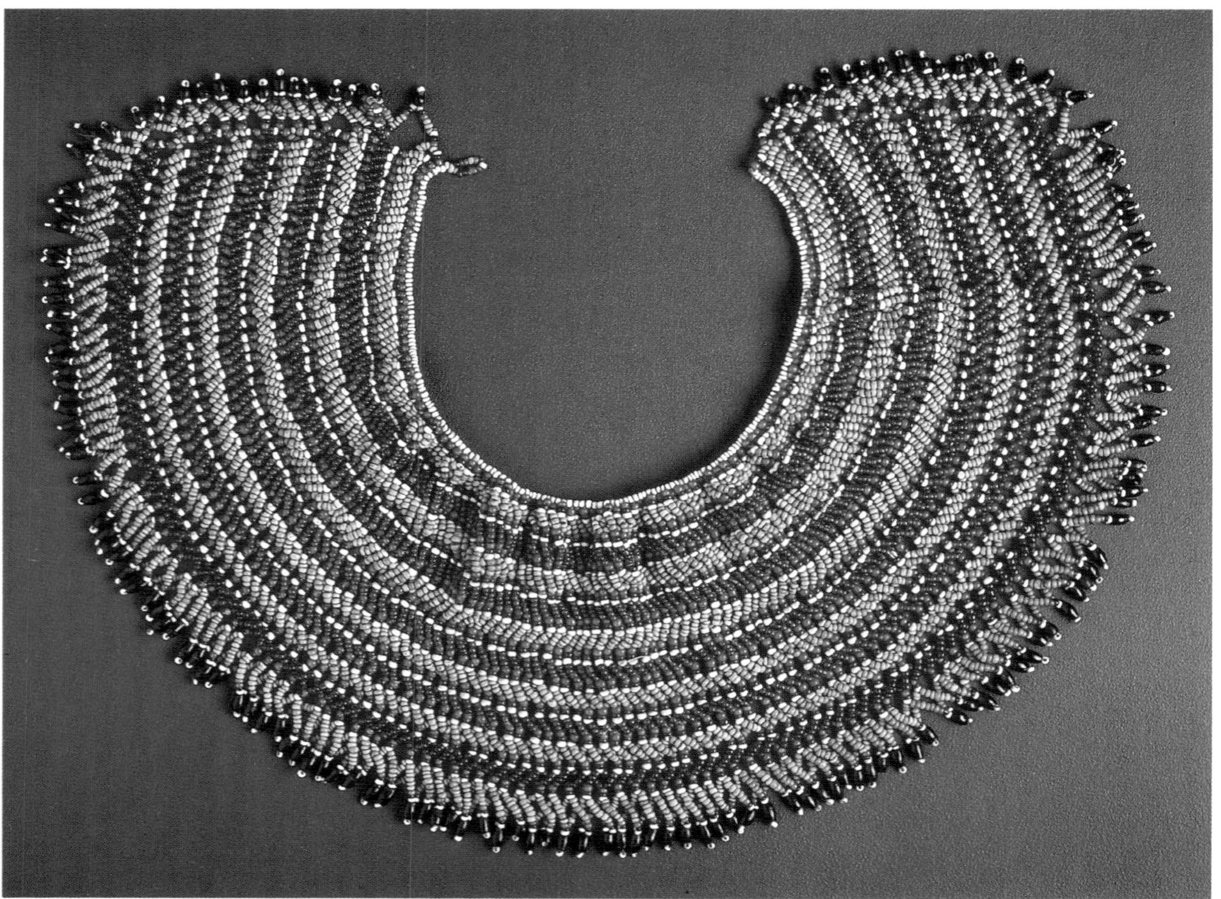

11

South Nguni, Mfengu
late 19th century / early 20th century

left:
11. Broad collar
early 20th century
37 x 49cm (laid out)

right:
anti-clockwise
12. Collar
width of band: 4cm, diameter: 18cm

13. Broad collar
width of band: 8.5cm, diameter: 28cm

14. Collar
width of band: 4cm, diameter: 32cm

15. Open-work waistband
78 x 3.5cm

16. Waistband
84 x 5cm

17. Headpiece
width: 7cm, diameter: 22cm

18. Necklace
length: 86cm

19. Beaded leather bracelet
width: 4.5cm, diameter: 10cm

Provenance for all the above:
Alfred John Gregory (1851–1927), who lived at the Cape between 1891 and 1914 and served as Medical Officer of Health for the Cape Colony between 1901 and 1910.
See DSAB, vol. 5.

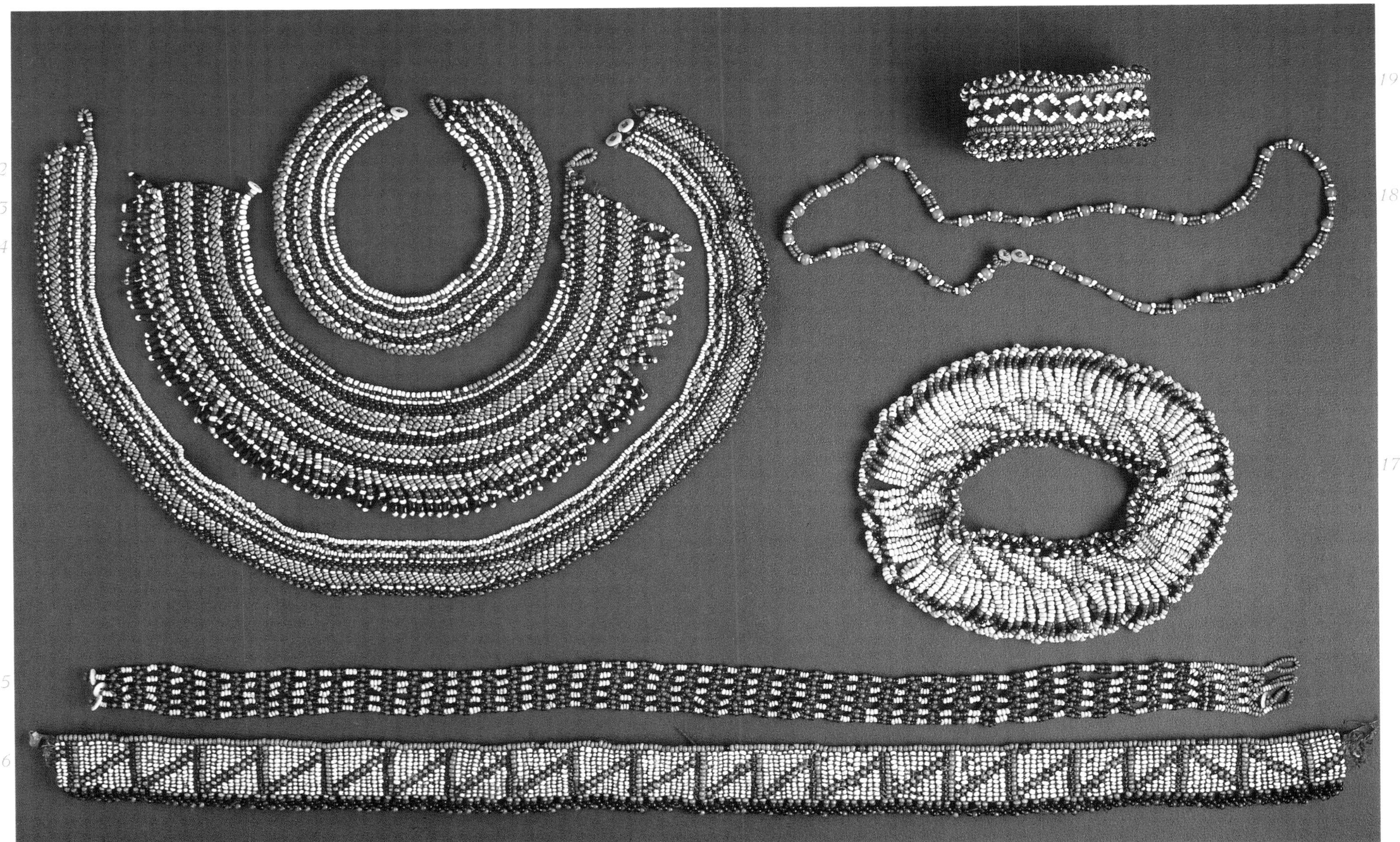
12
13
14
15
16
17
18
19

20

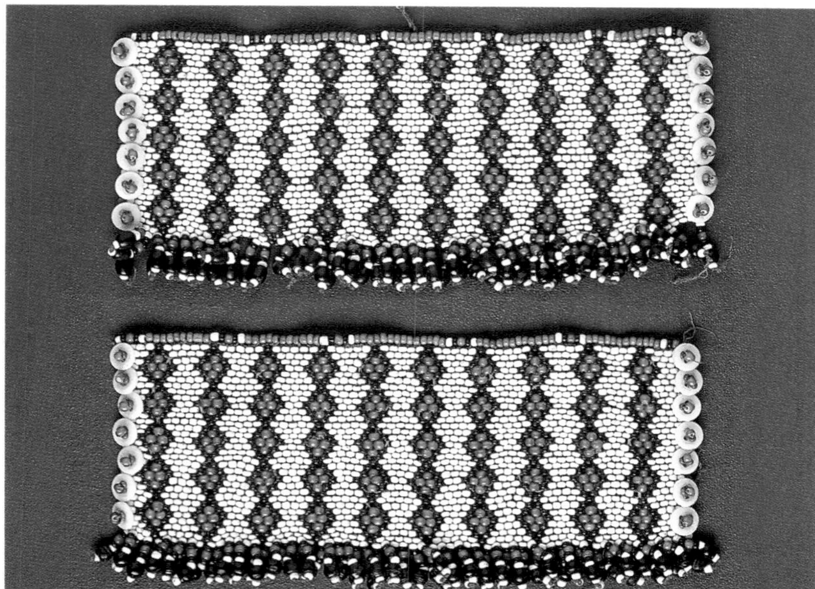

21

South Nguni, Mfengu
late 19th century / early 20th century

left:
20. Waistband and apron panel
panel: 13 x 25cm, length of waistband: 64.5cm

21. Pair of anklets
10 x 23cm each

Provenance for the above two pieces: Alfred John Gregory (1851–1927), who lived at the Cape between 1891 and 1914 and served as Medical Officer of Health for the Cape Colony between 1901 and 1910. See DSAB, vol. 5.

right:
22. Long panel with fringe
68 x 12cm

23. Neckpiece
overall length: 116cm

following two pages:
left:
24. Tasselled waistband and apron panel
panel: 12.5 x 24cm, waistband: 56 x 6cm

right:
25. Fringed waistband and apron panel
panel: 14 x 23cm, waistband: 61 x 7cm

Provenance: Alfred John Gregory (1851–1927), who lived at the Cape between 1891 and 1914 and served as Medical Officer of Health for the Cape Colony between 1901 and 1910. See DSAB, vol. 5.

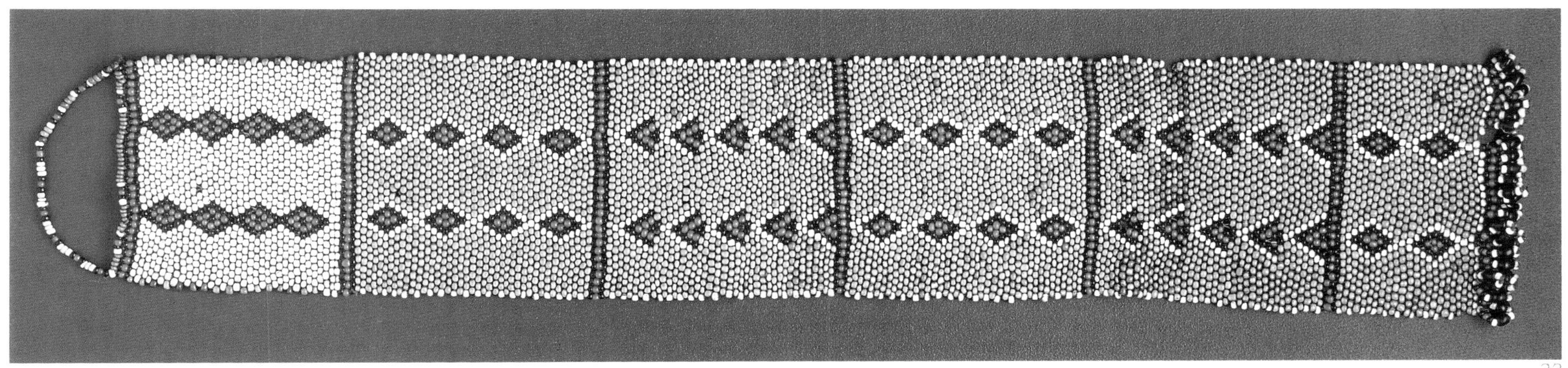

22

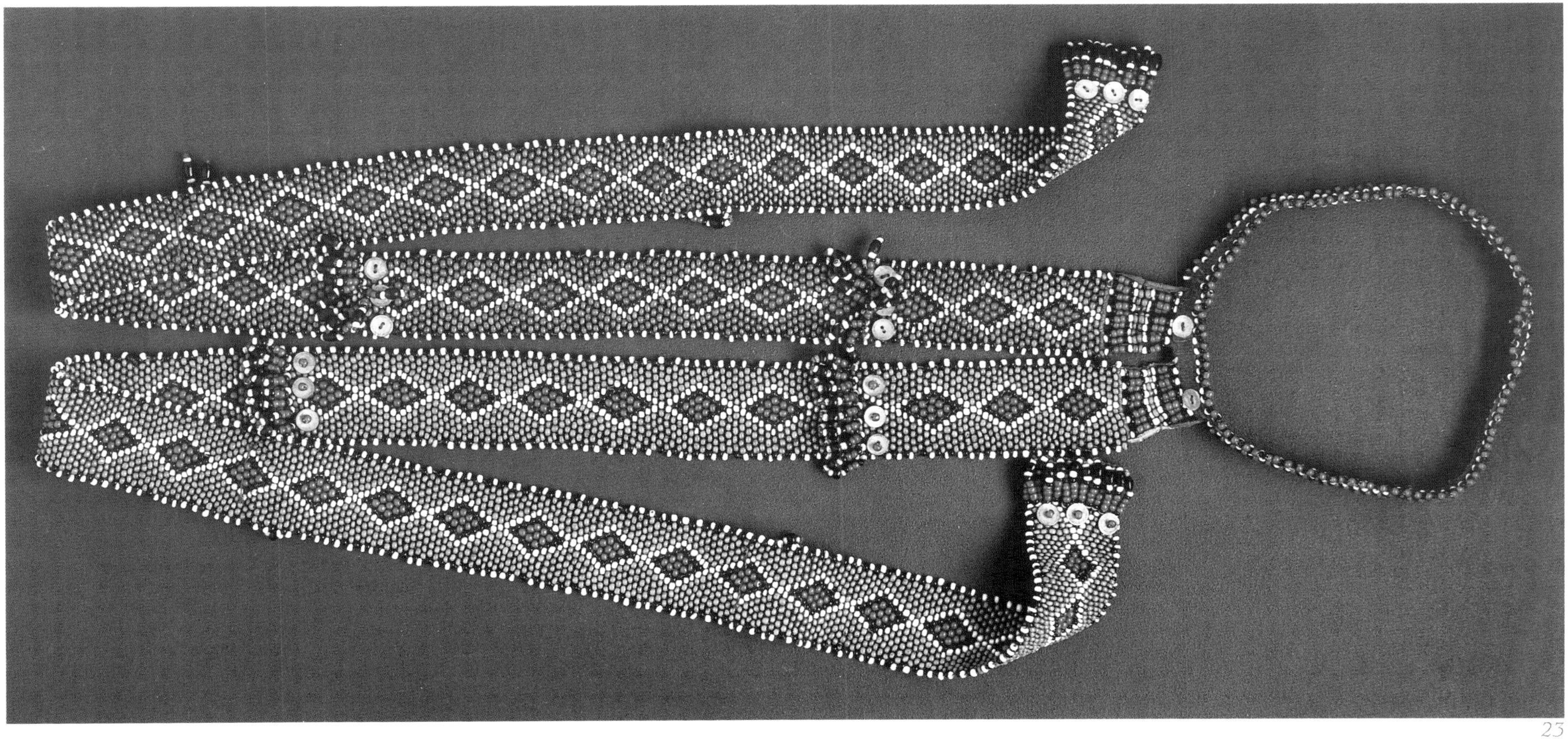

23

24

25

26

South Nguni
early 20th century

left:
Beaded gourd
26. *height: 19cm, width: 13cm*

right: clockwise
Beaded gourd snuff containers

27. Mfengu, *height: 11cm, width: 6.5cm*

28. *height: 12cm, width: 8.5cm*

29. *height: 13cm, width: 8cm*

30. Mfengu, *height: 11.5cm, width: 7cm*

31. *height: 10cm, width: 7cm*

32. *height: 5cm, width 6.5cm*

27

28

29

32

31

30

detail, no. 33

South Nguni, Mfengu
late 19th century / early 20th century

left:
detail, no. 33

right:
33. Beaded blanket cape
120 x 140cm (open), 100 x 140cm (top folded over)

following pages:
left:
34. Beaded blanket skirt
90 x 160cm (laid out)

cf. E.M. Shaw and N.J. van Warmelo, 'Material culture of the Cape Nguni', *Annals of the S.A. Museum*, vol. 58(4), p. 535, pl. 80(5).

right:
35. Beaded blanket cape
150 x 150cm

Provenance for the above two pieces: Alfred John Gregory (1851–1927), who lived at the Cape between 1891 and 1914 and served as Medical Officer of Health for the Cape Colony between 1901 and 1910. See DSAB, vol. 5.

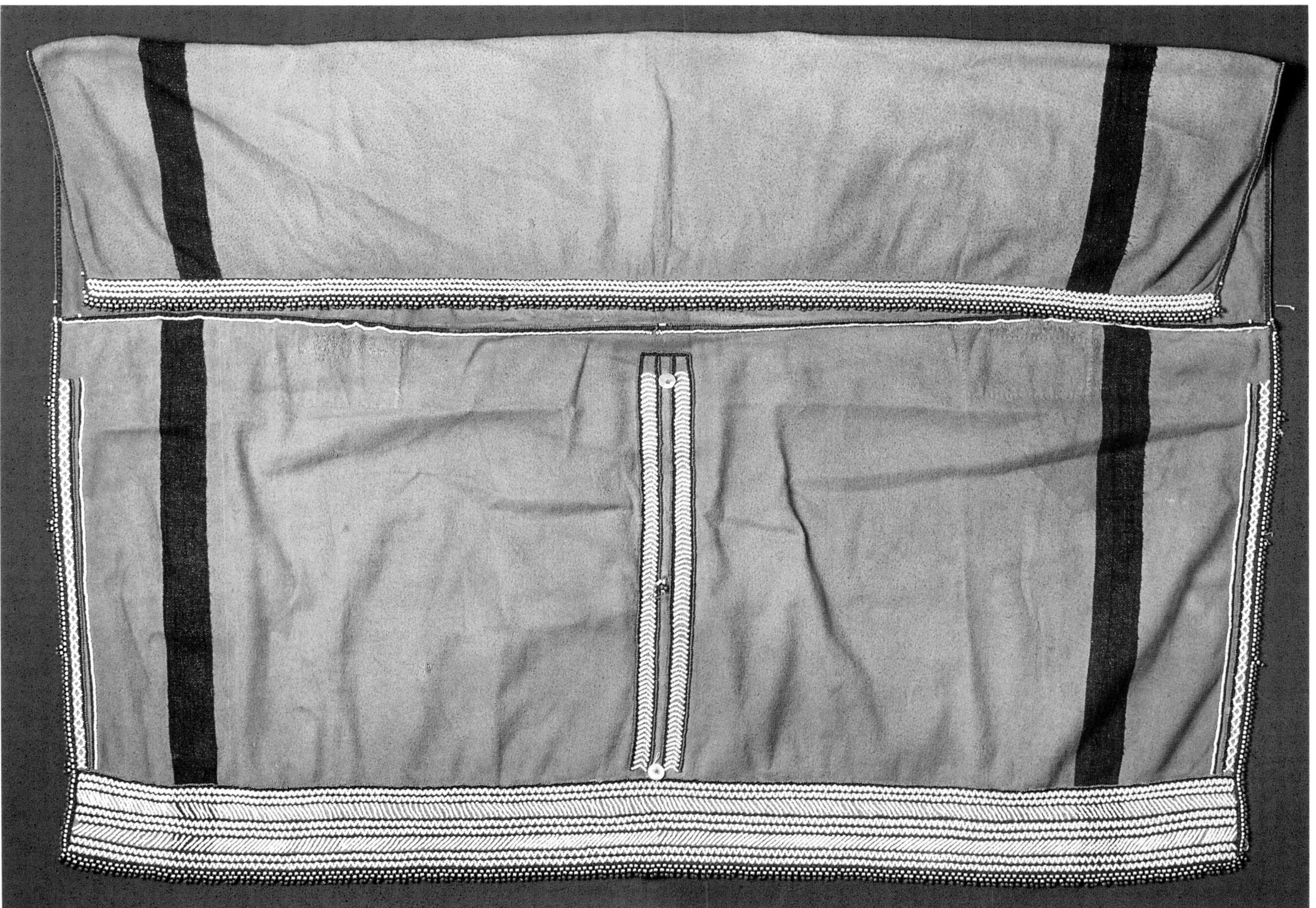

33

34

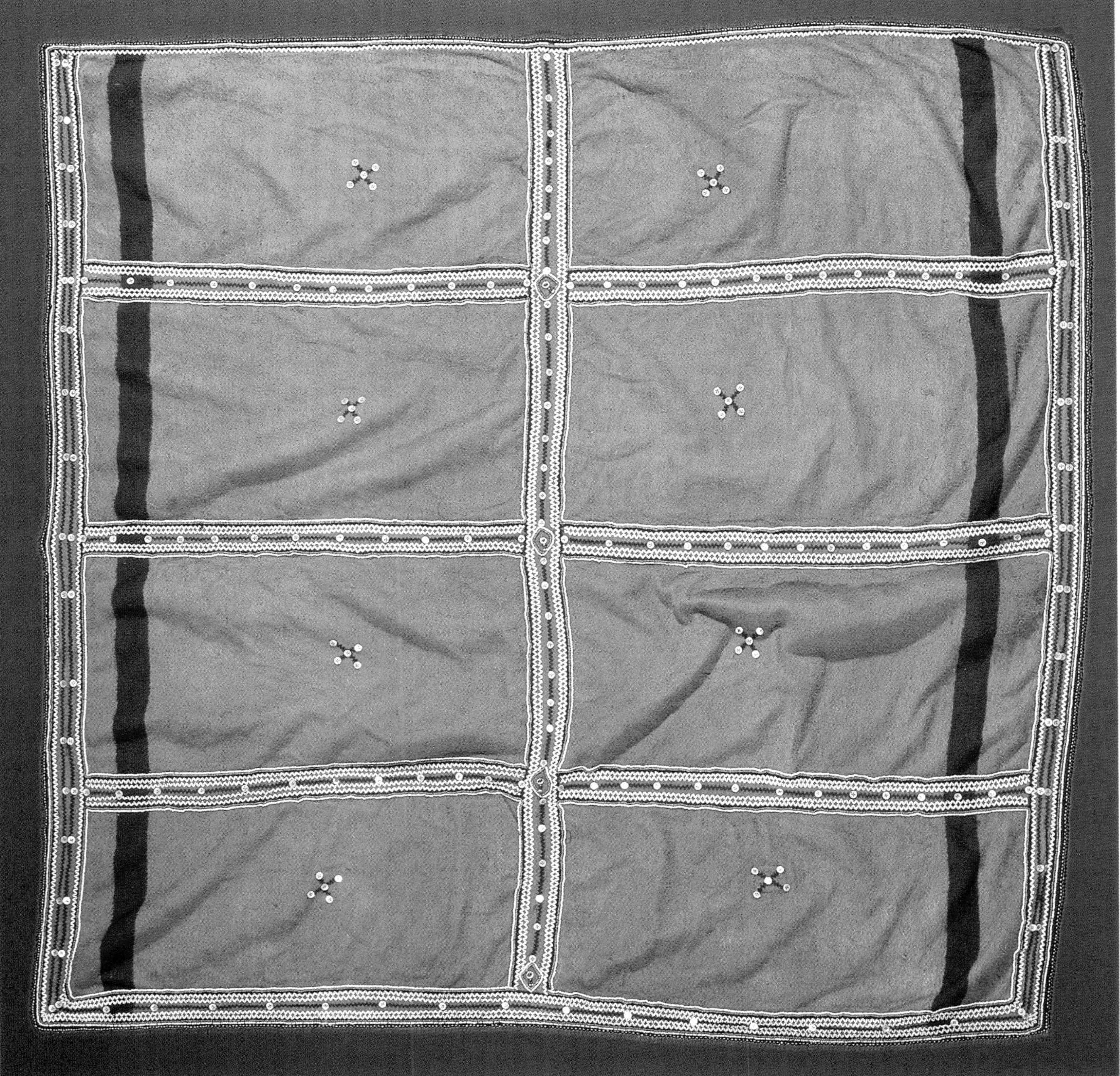

35

detail, no. 36

left:
detail, no. 36

right:
36. Drakensberg region
Beaded cloth
second half 19th century
66 x 86cm

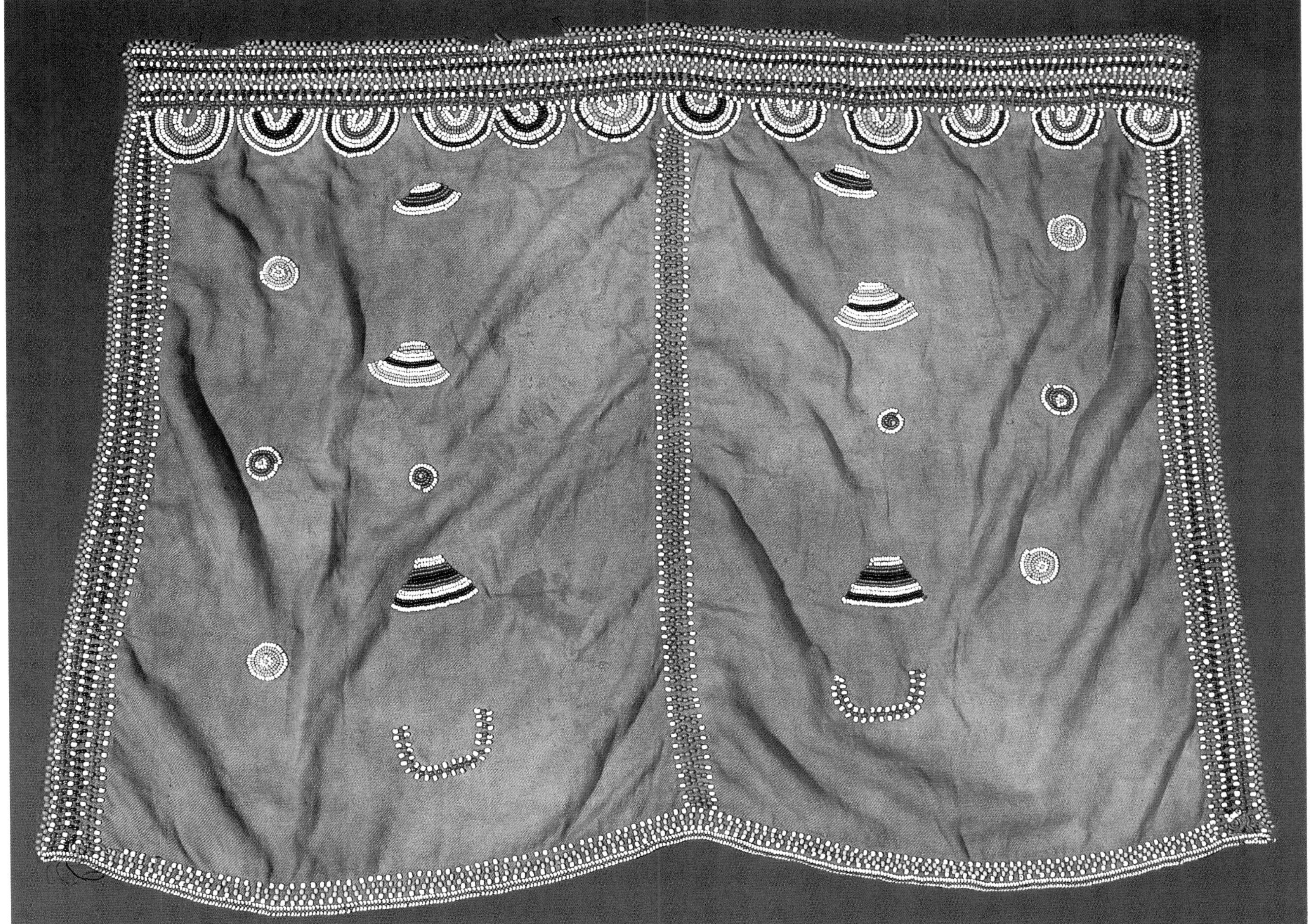

36

detail, no. 37

left:
detail, no. 37

right:
37. Drakensberg region
Beaded cloth
second half 19th century
100 x 100cm (open), 80 x 100cm (top folded over)

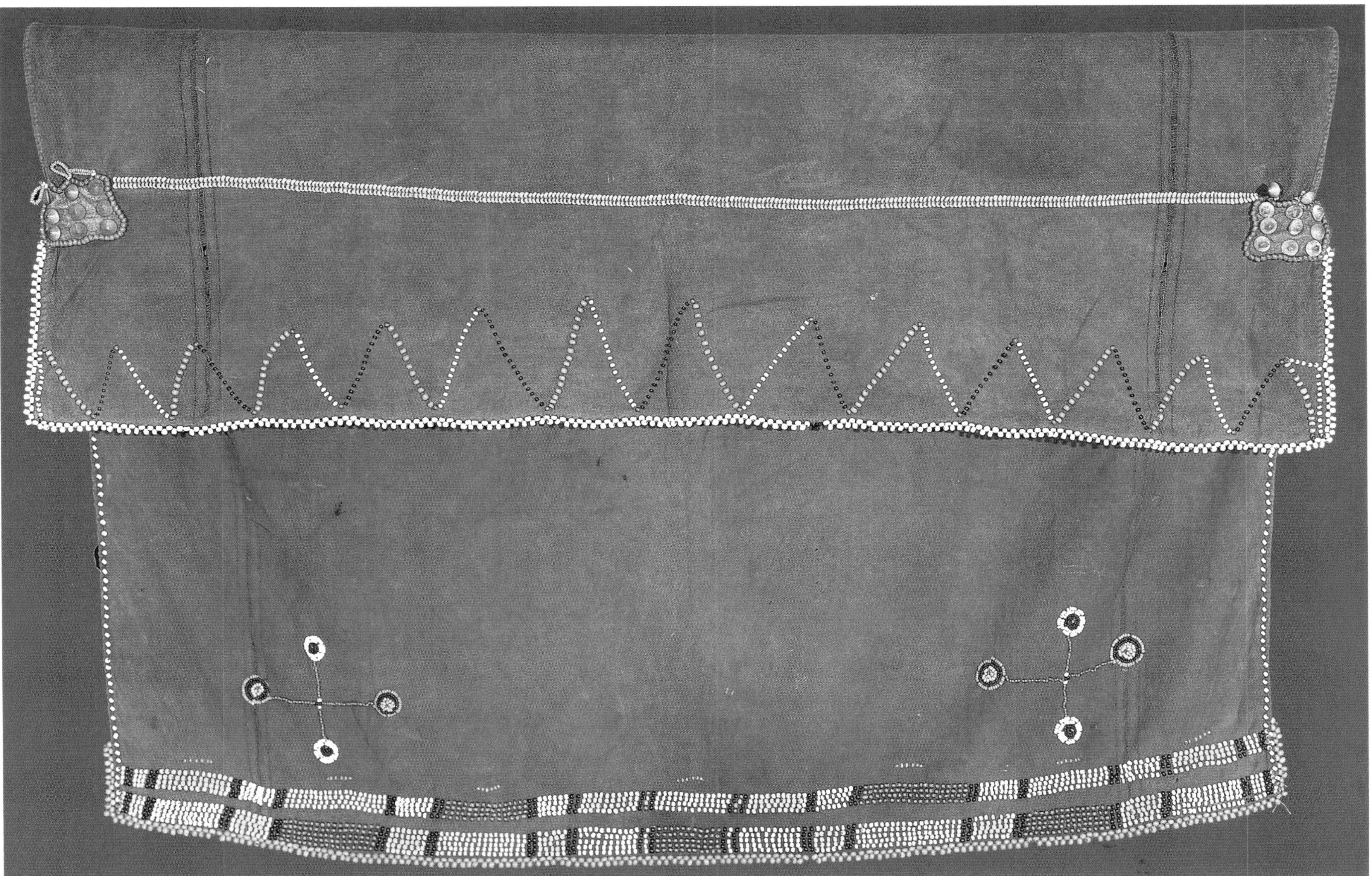

57

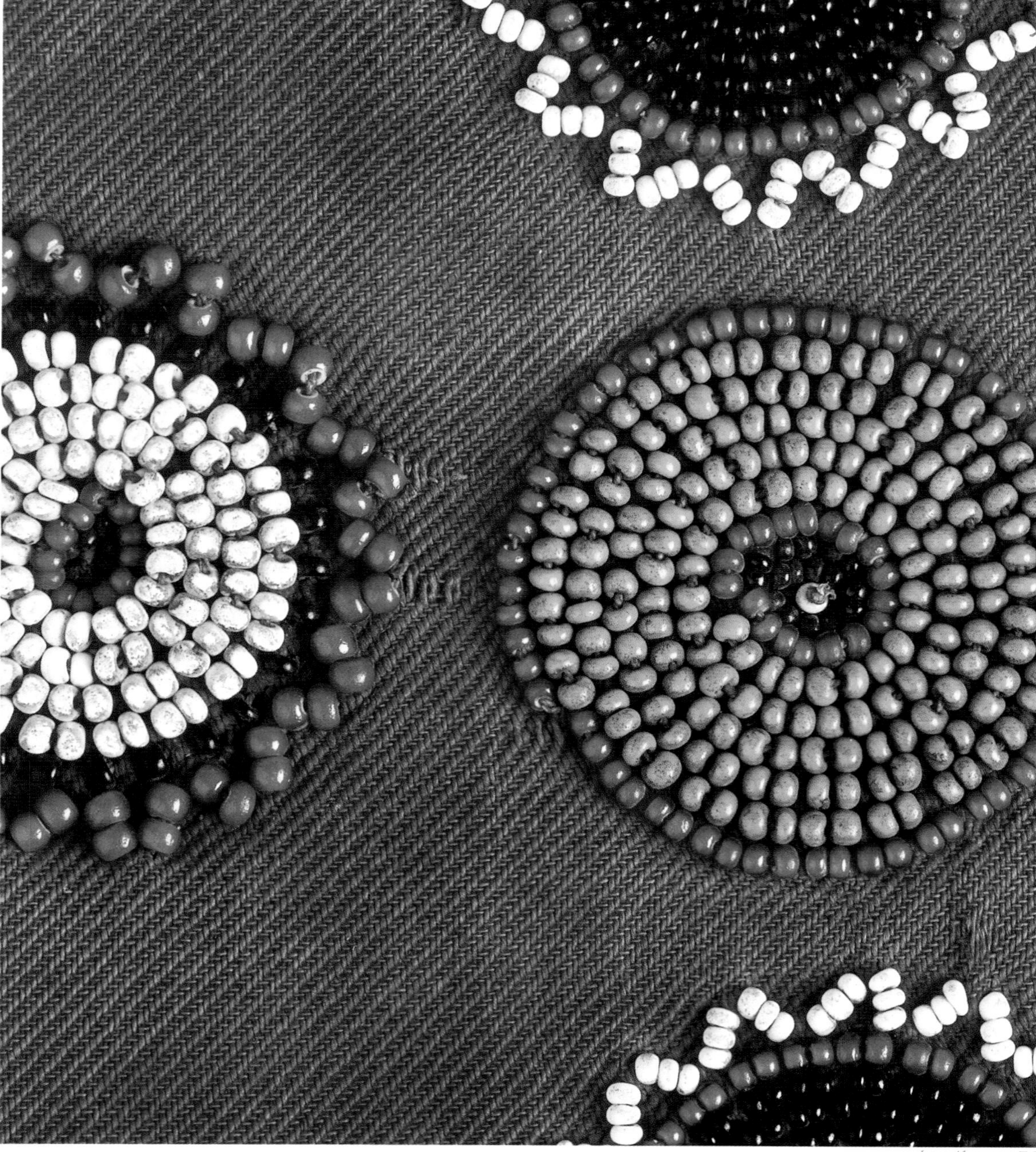

detail, no. 38

left:
detail, no. 38

right:
38. Drakensberg region
Beaded cloth
second half 19th century
80 x 101cm

38

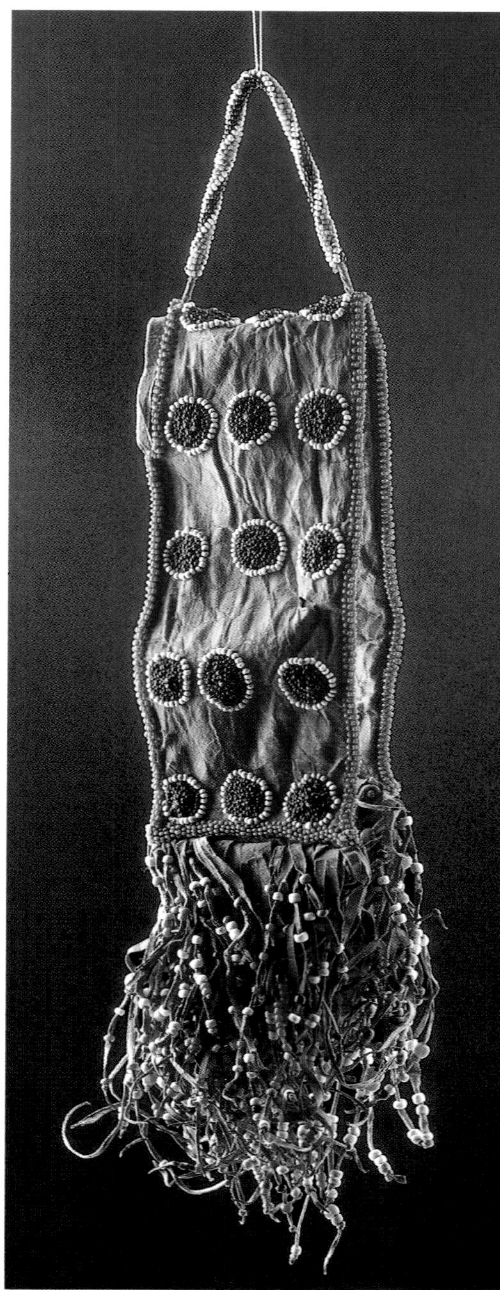
39

left and right:

39. Drakensberg region, probably South Sotho
Beaded leather bag with beaded leather strap and fringe
late 19th century
10 x 75cm (laid out)

Provenance: Alfred John Gregory (1851–1927), who lived at the Cape between 1891 and 1914 and served as Medical Officer of Health for the Cape Colony between 1901 and 1910. See DSAB, vol. 5.

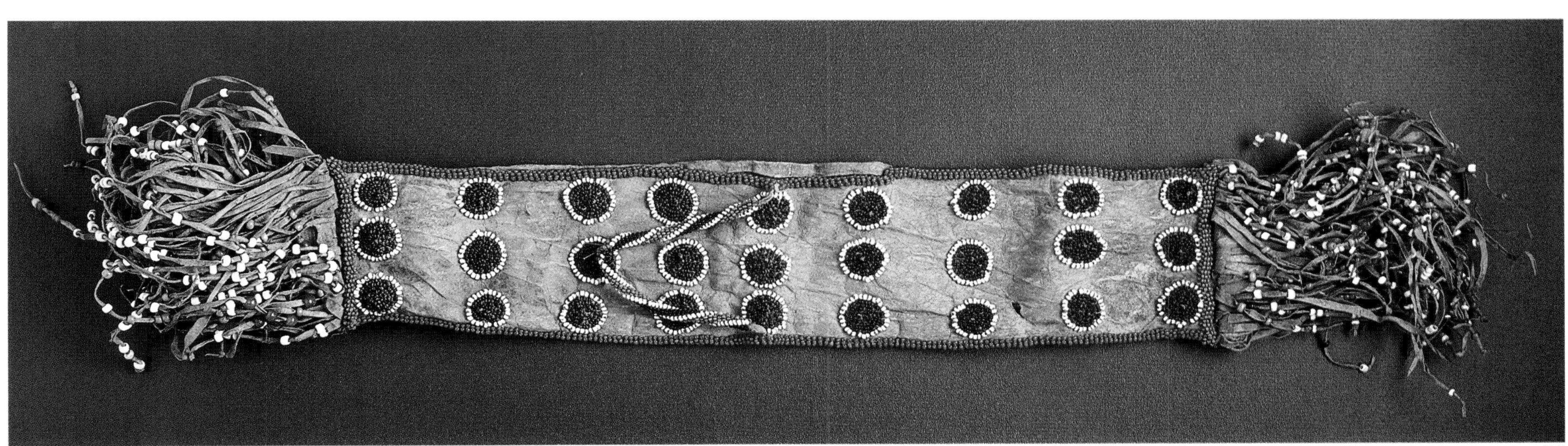

59

40

South-east Africa
late 19th century

left:
40. Apron panel
30 x 34cm

right:
41. Long panel with fringe
88 x 11.5cm

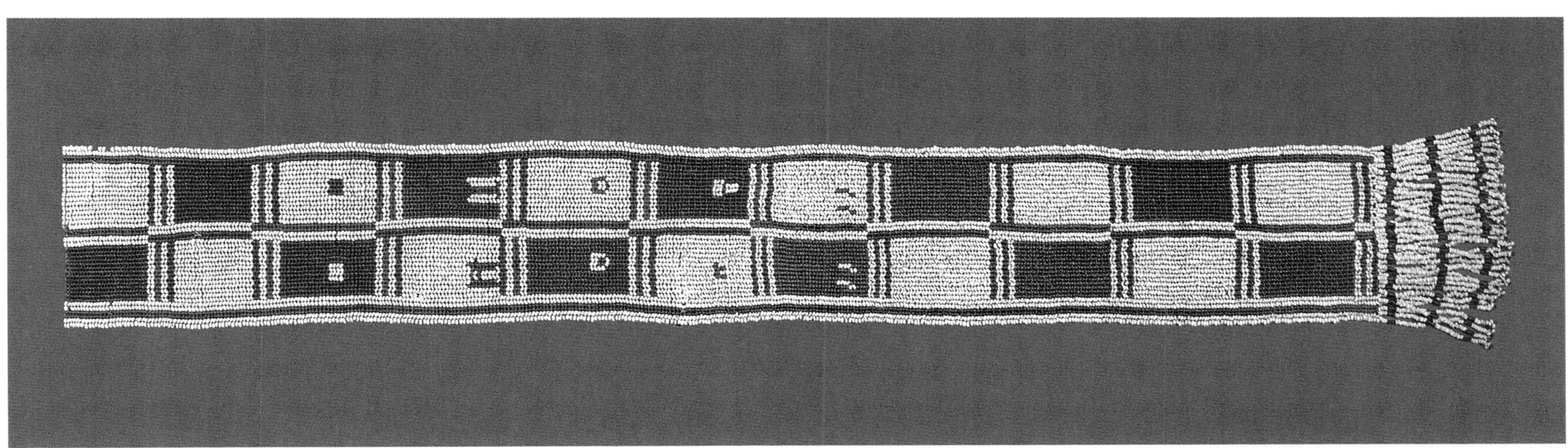

41

42

left:

42. South-east Africa
Beaded gourd snuff container
late 19th century
height: 13cm, width: 9.5cm

right:

43. Probably South Sotho
Beaded leather apron
mid 19th century
22.5 x 20cm

See M. Carey, *Beads and beadwork of East and South Africa*, p. 39; and E.M. Shaw and N.J. van Warmelo, 'The material culture of the Cape Nguni', *Annals of S.A. Museum*, vol. 58(4), p. 513, pl. 70(2,3).

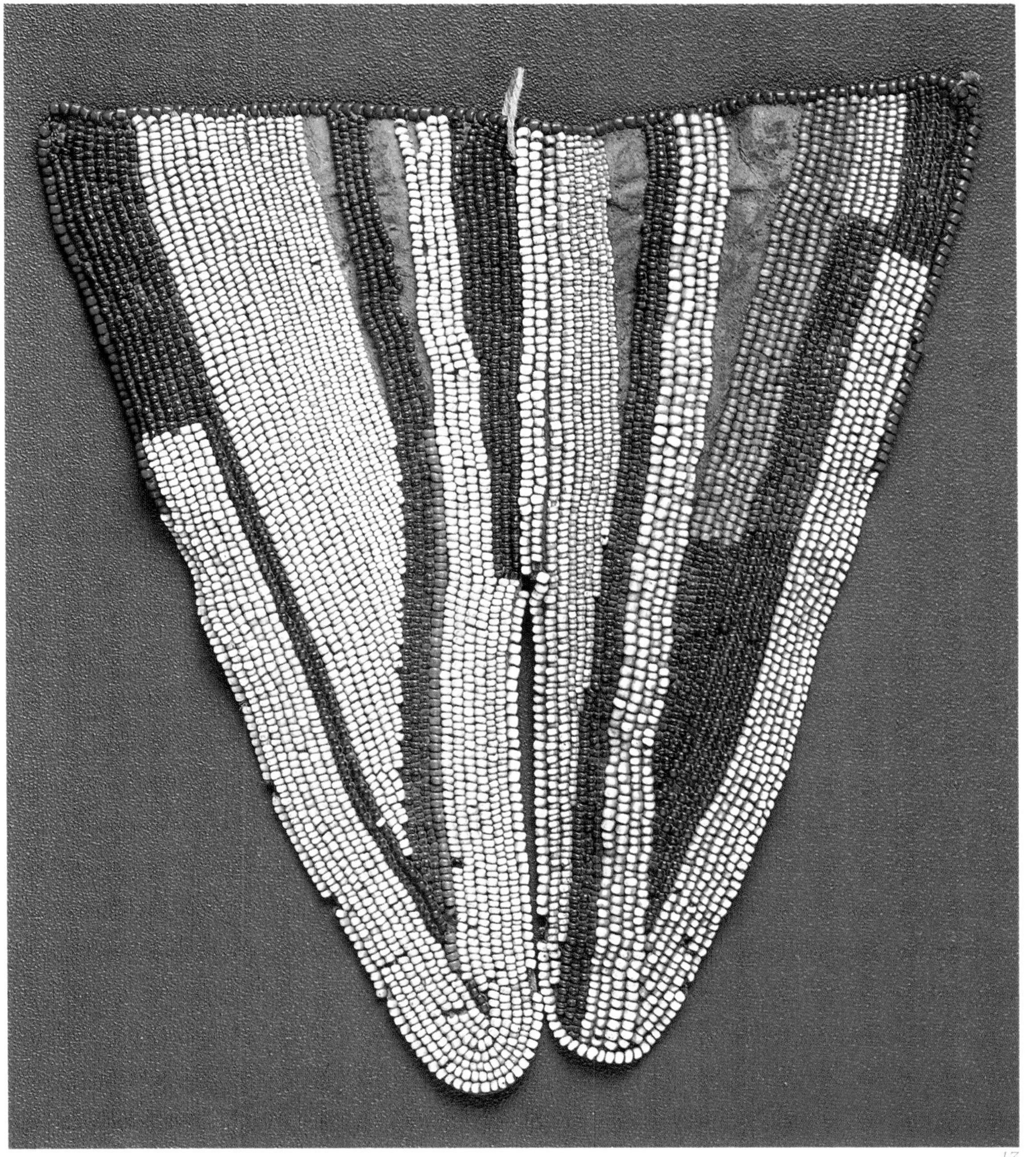

43

detail, no. 44

left:
detail, no. 44

right:
44. Drakensberg region, probably South Sotho
Beaded leather-backed panel with fringes
late 19th century
56 x 26cm (excluding tassles)

44

detail, no. 45

left:
detail, no. 45

right:
45. Drakensberg region
Long panel with fringe
late 19th century
78 x 10.5cm

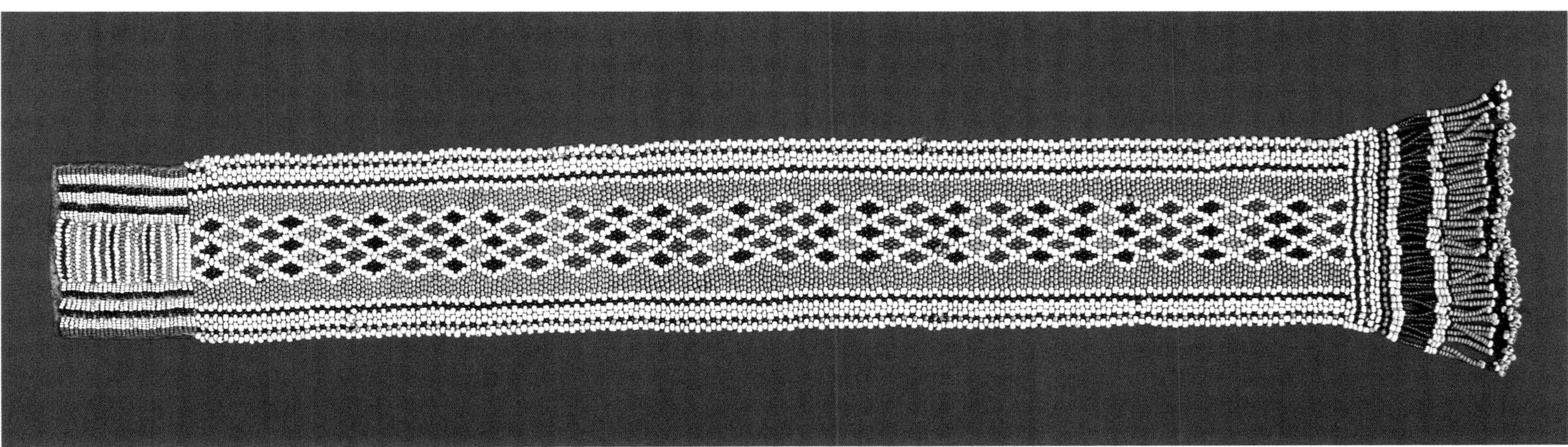

45

detail, no. 46

left:
detail, no. 46

right:
46. South Nguni or South Sotho
Beaded cloth-backed waistband with clasp
late 19th century
64 x 6cm (including clasp)

47. South Nguni or South Sotho
Beaded cloth-backed waistband with clasp
late 19th century
72 x 5cm (including clasp)

48. South-east Africa
Waistband
late 19th century
73 x 3cm

49. South Sotho
Fringed waistband
late 19th century
57 x 7cm

46

47

48

49

50

left:
50. Drakensberg region
Panel
late 19th century
panel: 6 x 22.5cm

cf. to the attachment on the fertility figure in the S.A. Museum collected in Lesotho in 1904, illustrated in *Evocations of the child: fertility figures of the southern African region*, Cape Town, 1998, p. 44, fig. 4.

right:
51. Drakensberg region, probably South Sotho
Beaded bag
late 19th century
17 x 22cm

51

52

left:

52. Probably North Nguni
Two-roll waistband and fringed apron panel
late 19th century
apron: 14 x 21cm, length of waistband: 75cm

right:

North Nguni
late 19th century

53. Three-roll waistband with fringe in alternating sections
89 x 10cm

54. Five-roll waistband
76 x 5cm

55. Five-roll waistband
73 x 5cm

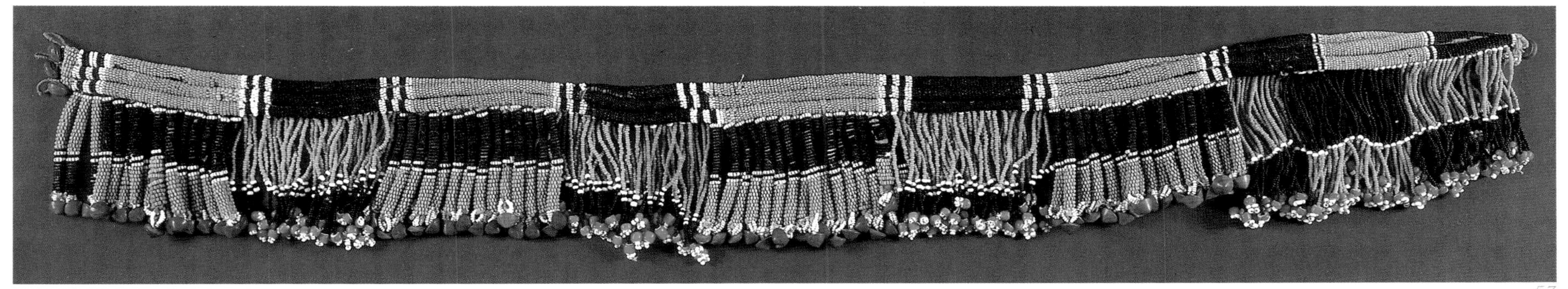

53

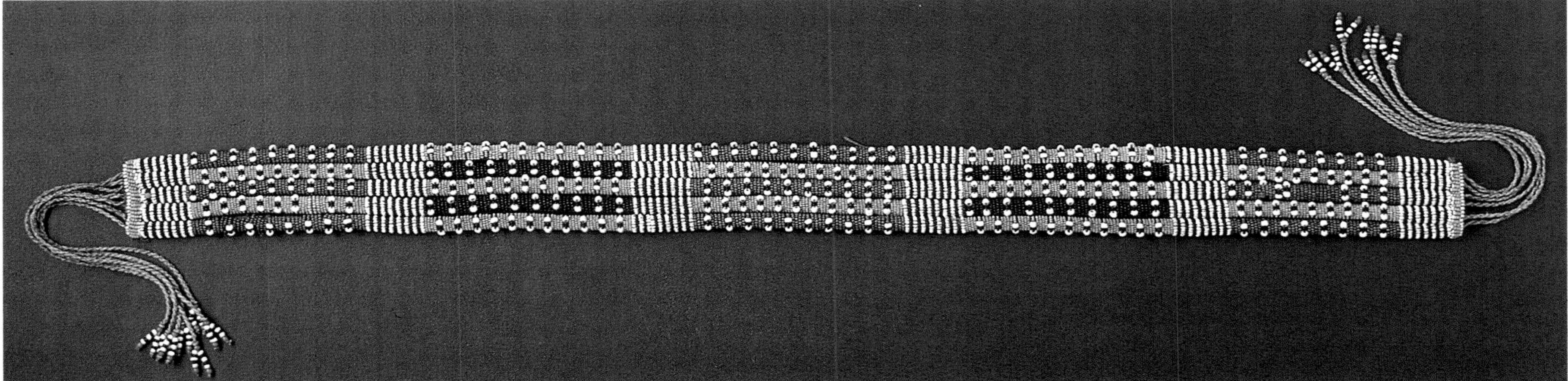

54

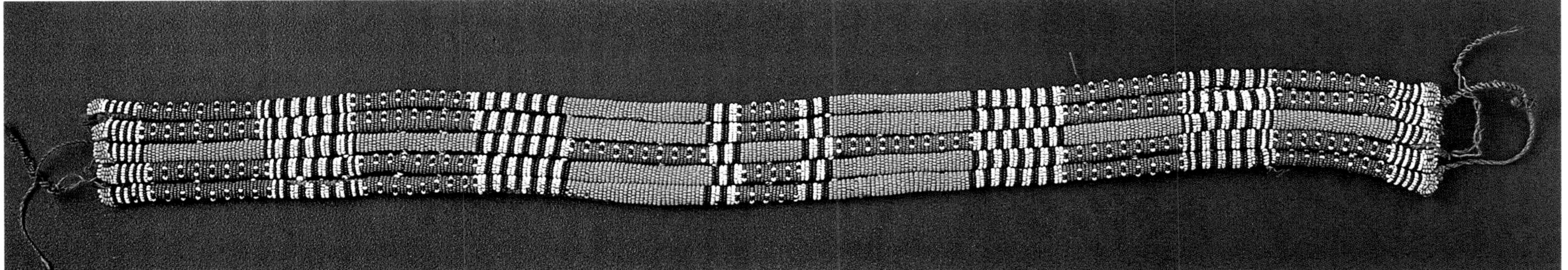

55

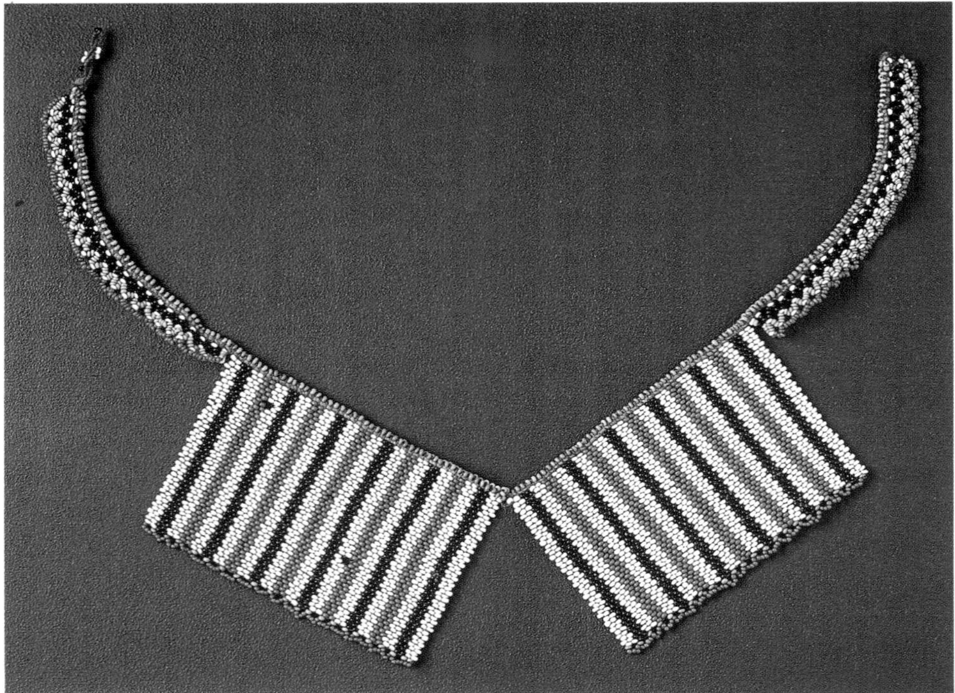

56

57

left:
Drakensberg region
late 19th century

56. Neckpiece
each panel: 7 x 11cm

57. Neckpiece
each panel: 9 x 7cm

right:
58. Fringed apron panel
18 x 28cm

58

59

left:
59. Southern Drakensberg region, probably Hlubi
Beaded leather-backed panel
early 20th century
12.5 x 20.5cm

right:
60. Southern Drakensberg region, probably Hlubi
Bridal veil
late 19th century
21 x 22cm

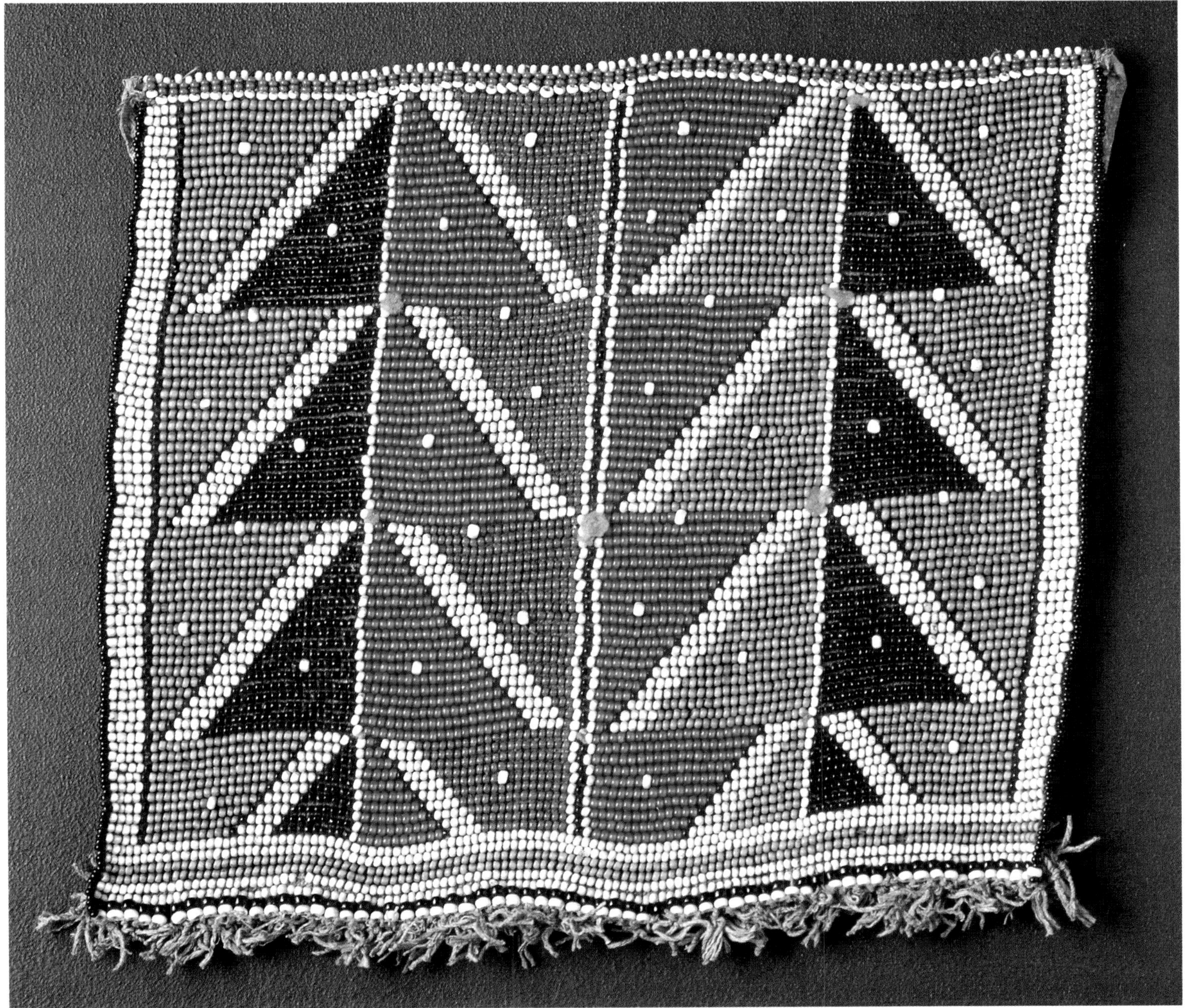

60

61

Drakensberg region, possibly South Sotho
Bags
late 19th century

left:
61. *bag: 27 x 25cm (bottom width)*

right:
62. *bag: 15.5 x 24cm (bottom width)*

63. *bag: 8 x 16cm (bottom width)*

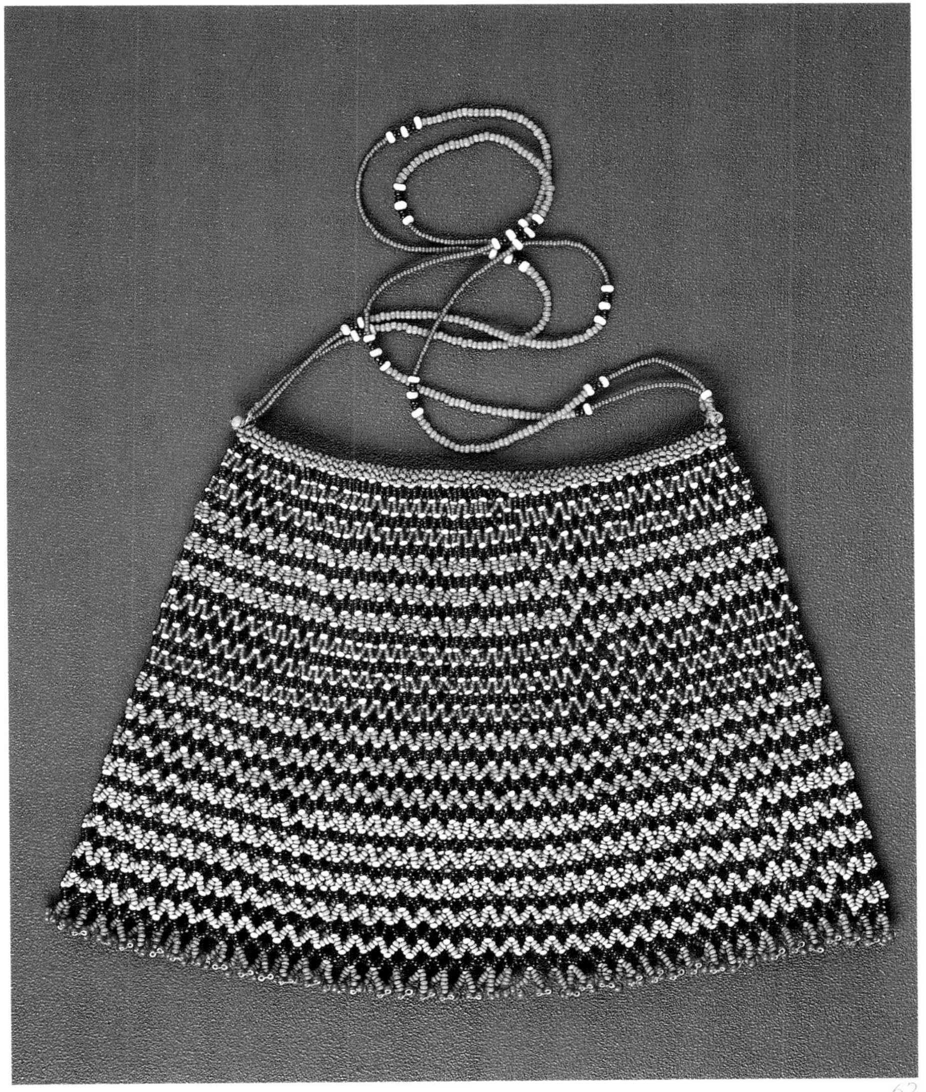

62

63

64

left:
64. North Nguni
Neckpiece
late 19th century
panel: 11 x 16cm

right:
South-east Africa
Beaded cloth-backed pouches
late 19th century

65. *9.5 x 13.5cm*

66. *12.5 x 13cm (closed)*

67. *12.5 x 11.5cm*

65

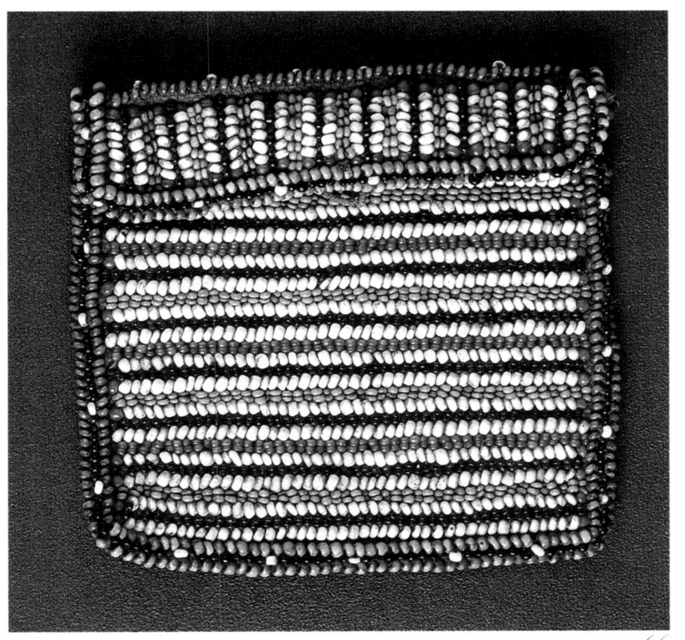
66

67

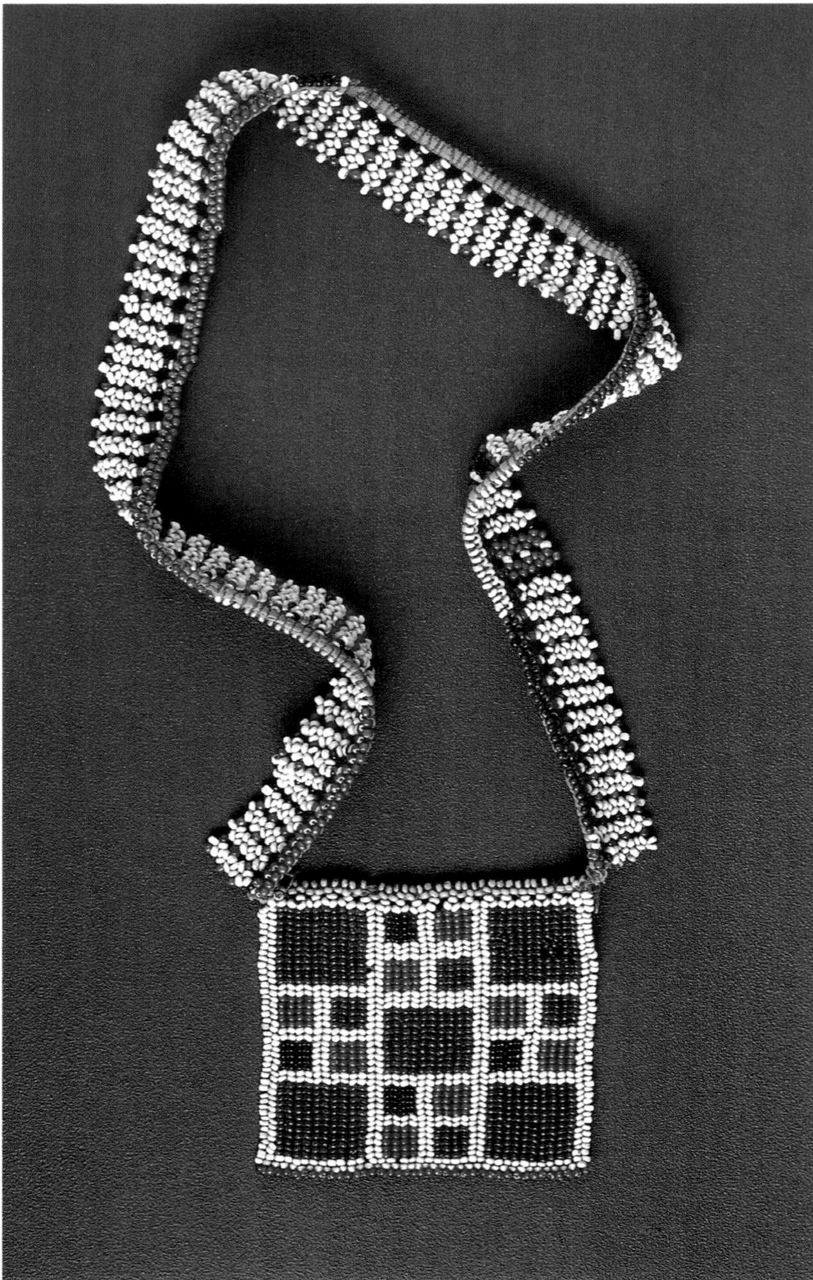

68

North Nguni
late 19th century

left:

68. Neckpiece
panel: 9 x 10cm, length of neckband: 76cm

right:
top to bottom

69. Neckpiece
36 x 5.5cm

70. Neckpiece
panel: 20 x 3.5cm

71. Long panel
51 x 8cm

72. Neckpiece
long panel: 50 x 3.5cm, four small panels: 3 x 5cm each

73. Long panel
67 x 13cm

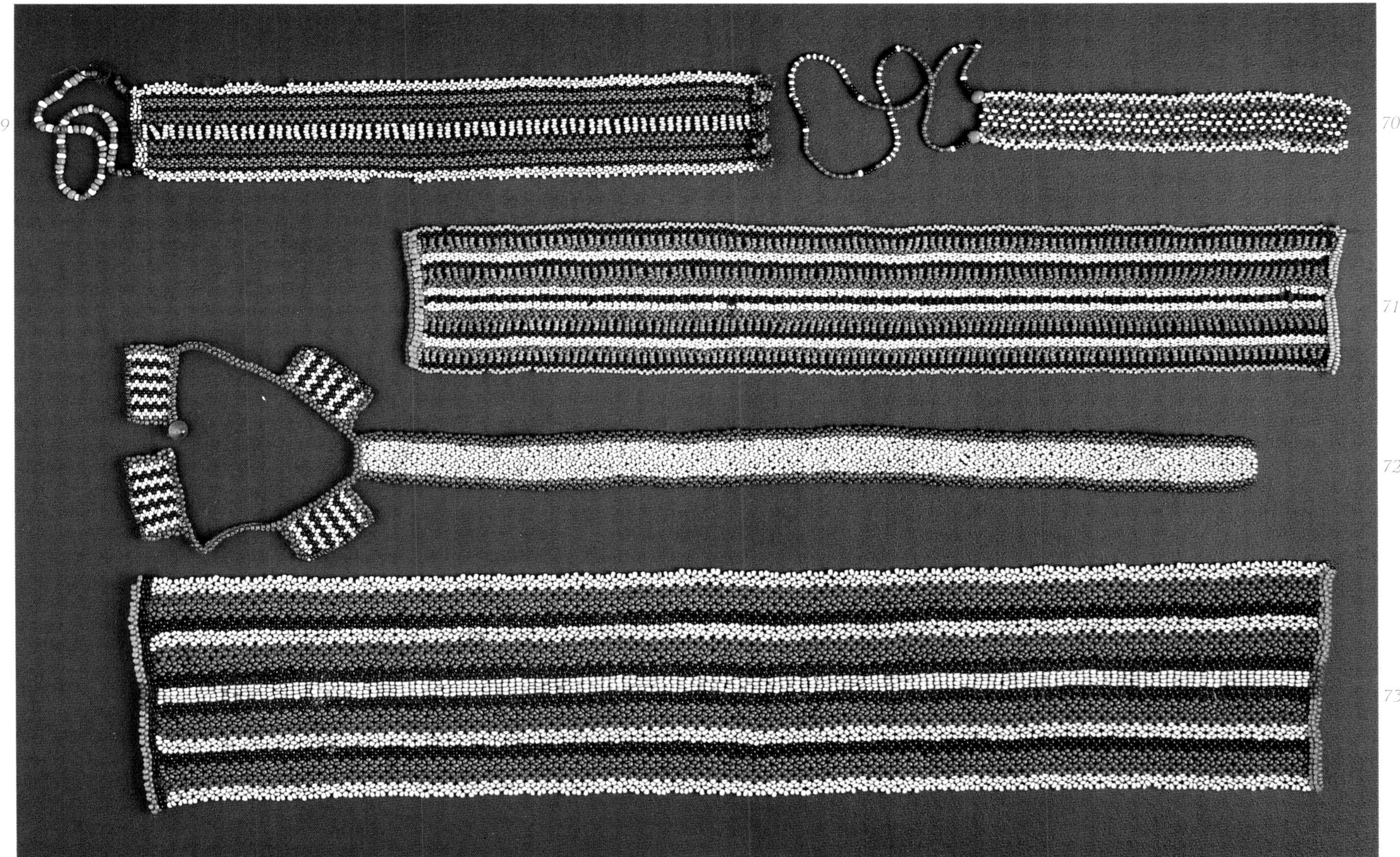
69
70
71
72
73

74

North Nguni
late 19th century

left:
74. Neckpiece
panel: 16 x 13cm

right:
75. Panel
16 x 20cm

75

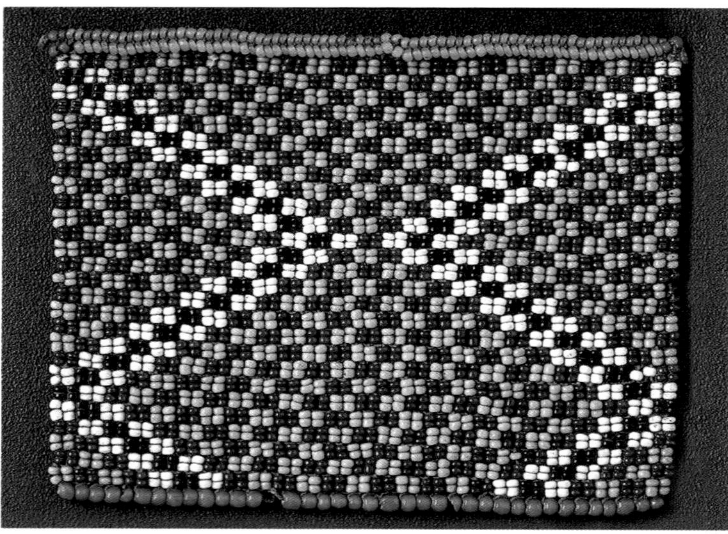

76

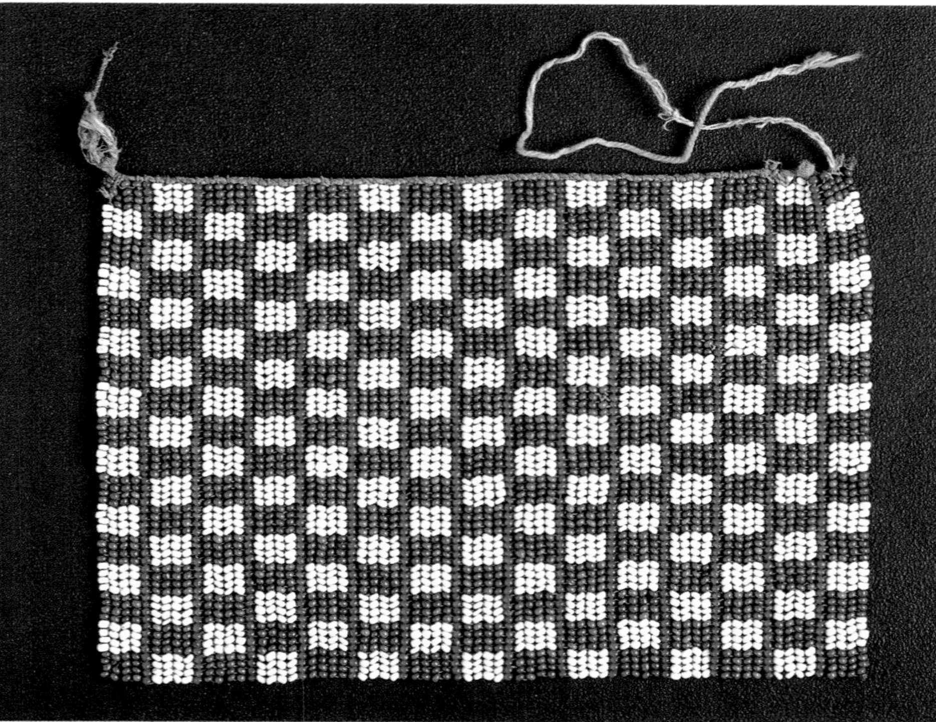

77

North Nguni
late 19th century

left:
76. Panel
10.5 x 13.5cm

77. Panel
13 x 19cm

right:
78. Five-roll waistband with apron panel
waistband: 84 x 6cm, panel: 8 x 14.5cm

79. Cloth-backed waistband
76 x 10cm

cf. stylistically to *Zulu treasures*, Durban, 1996, B1.

80. Waistband
75 x 4cm

cf. stylistically to *Zulu treasures*, Durban, 1996, B1.

81. Fringed waistband
60 x 5.5cm

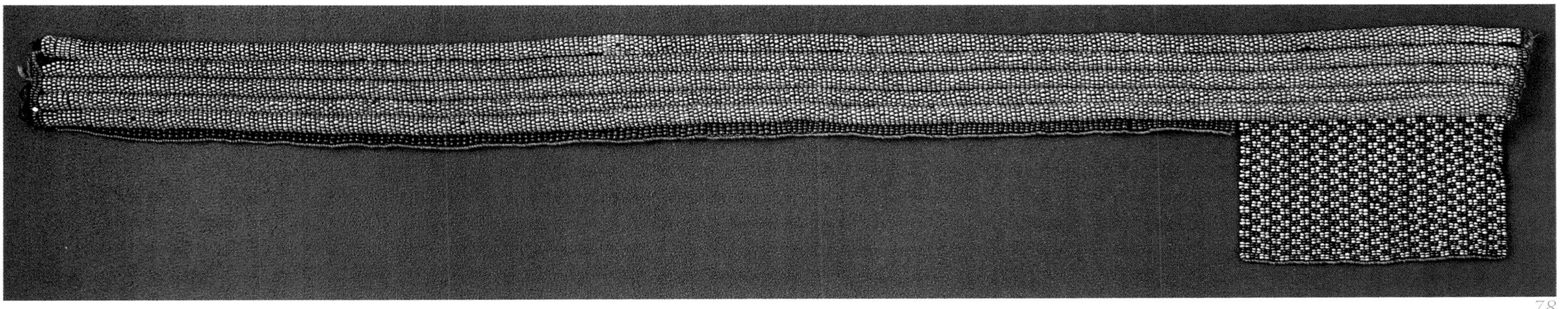

78

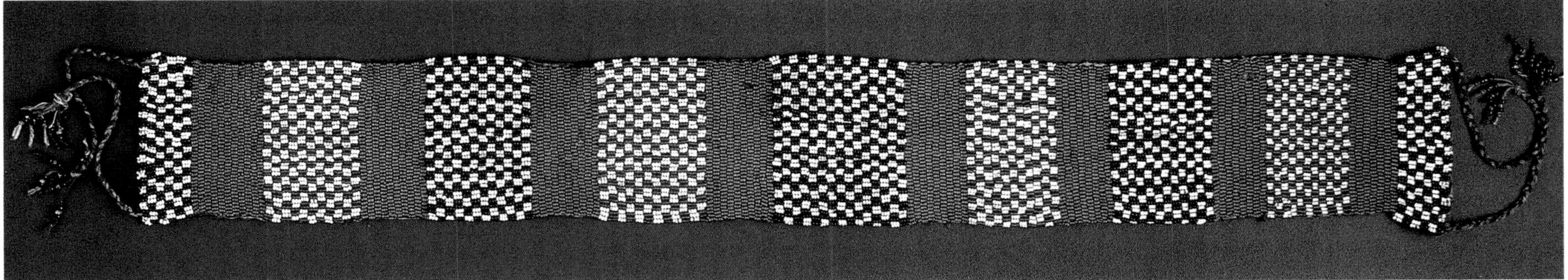

79

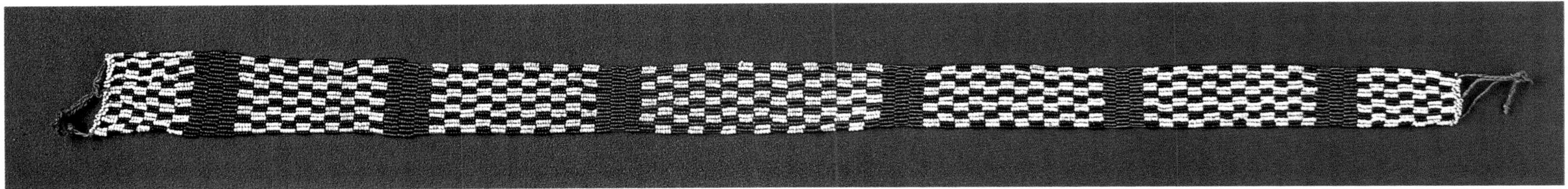

80

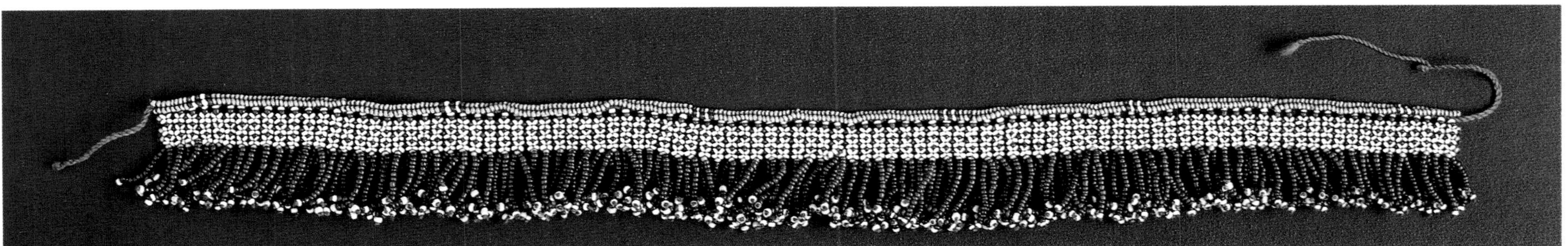

81

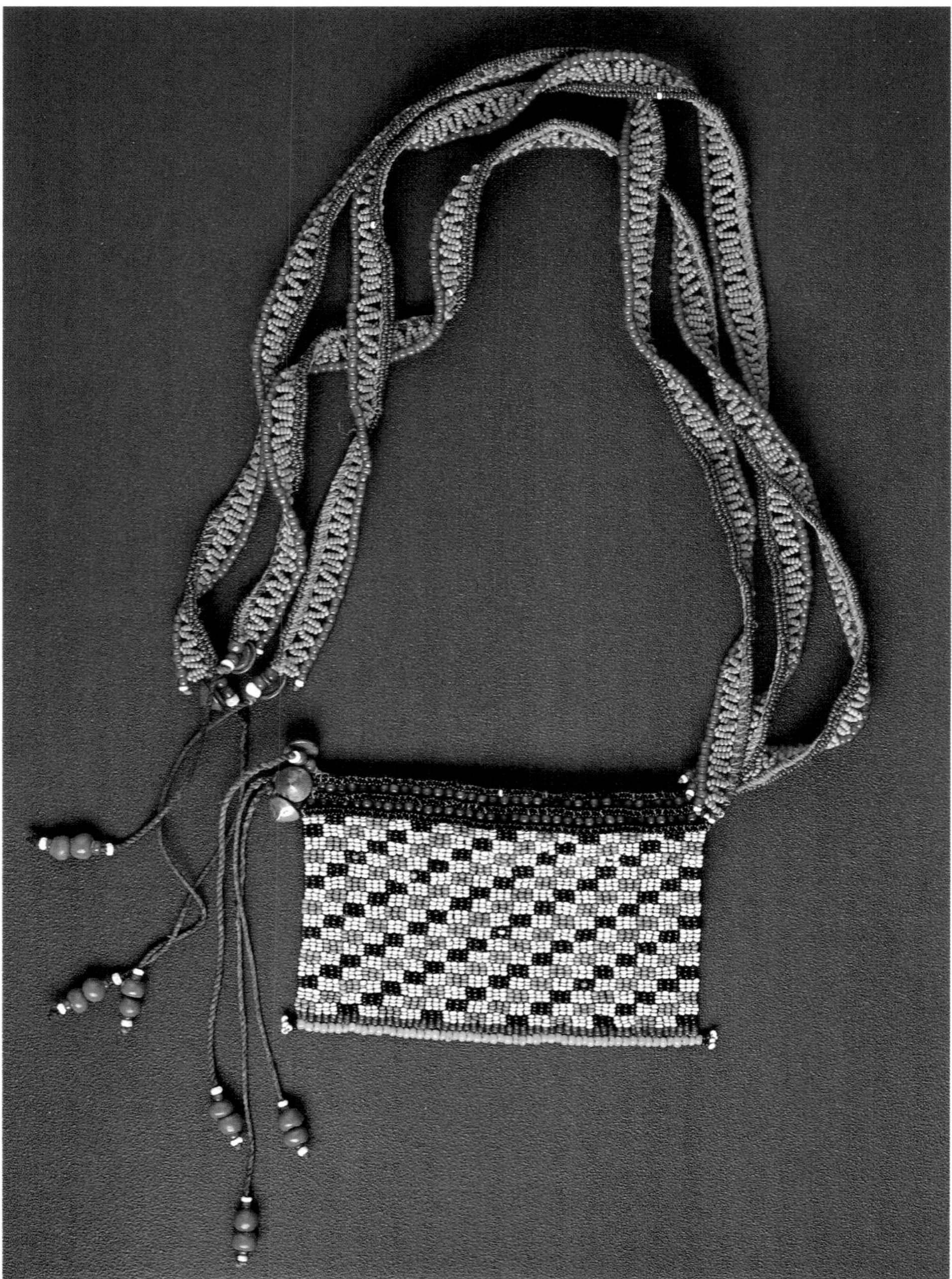

82

North Nguni
Neckpieces
late 19th century

left:
82. *panel: 9.3 x 14cm, straps: 59 x 1.5cm each*
cf. *Art and ambiguity*, Johannesburg, 1991, cat. no. 673, illus. pl. 38.

right:
83. *panel: 13.5cm x 10cm, length of strap: 23cm, length of tassels: 34cm*
cf. *Art and ambiguity*, Johannesburg, 1991, cat. no. 673, illus. pl. 38.

83

84

85

86

87

North Nguni
Beaded gourd snuff containers
late 19th century

left:
anti-clockwise

84. *height: 5.5cm, width: 4.5cm*

85. *height: 4cm, width: 4.5cm*
label inscribed: 'Isiyingo somncake / naematambo abazwe / afaniswa nezinzwane / ze nibule / Maritzburg Dec. 9. [18]90' and 'A. Burney / Zululand'

86. *height: 4.5cm, width: 4.5cm*

87. *height: 5cm, width: 6cm, length of strap: 36cm*

right:
clockwise

88. *height: 3.5cm, width: 4cm, length of strap: 13cm*

89. *height: 3.5cm, width: 4cm, length of strap: 17cm*
label inscribed: 'Amashungu. / 2. Snuff boxes / Maritzburg / July 8. [18]90' and 'A. Burney'

90. *height: 8.5cm, width: 8.5cm*

91. *height: 6cm, width: 6.5cm*
label inscribed: 'Umgqwako wamafuta / Grease Pot / May [18]91 / Maritzburg', 'A. Burney / Zululand'

92. *height: 6.5cm, width: 4cm*

93. *height: 4cm, width: 4.5cm, length of strap: 43cm*

88

89

90

93

91

92

94

North Nguni
late 19th century

left:
94. Beaded chrysalis snuff container
length: 4.5cm, length of strap: 76cm

right:
Beaded cylindrical snuff containers

95. *length: 10cm, length of strap: 88cm*
cf. H.P.N. Muller and J.F. Snelleman, *'L'Industrie des Cafres du sud-est de l'Afrique*, c.1892, pl. XI(15).

96. *length: 11.5cm, length of strap: 70cm*
cf. *Zulu treasures*, B131.

97. *length: 9.5cm*

98. *length: 11.5cm, length of strap: 70cm*
cf. *Art and ambiguity*, Johannesburg, 1991, cat. no. 455.

99. *length: 18cm*

100. *length: 9.5cm, length of strap: 56cm*

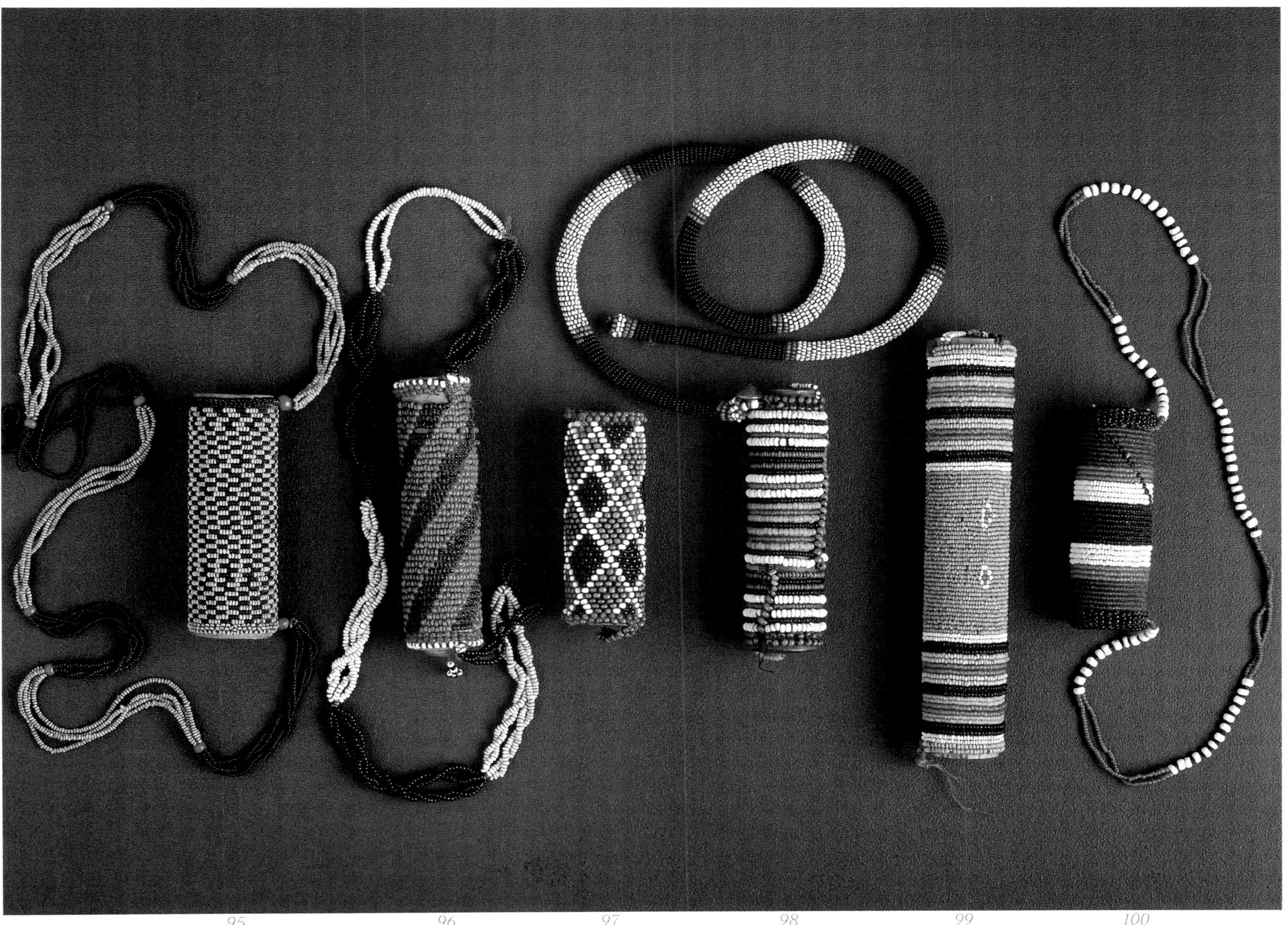

95 96 97 98 99 100

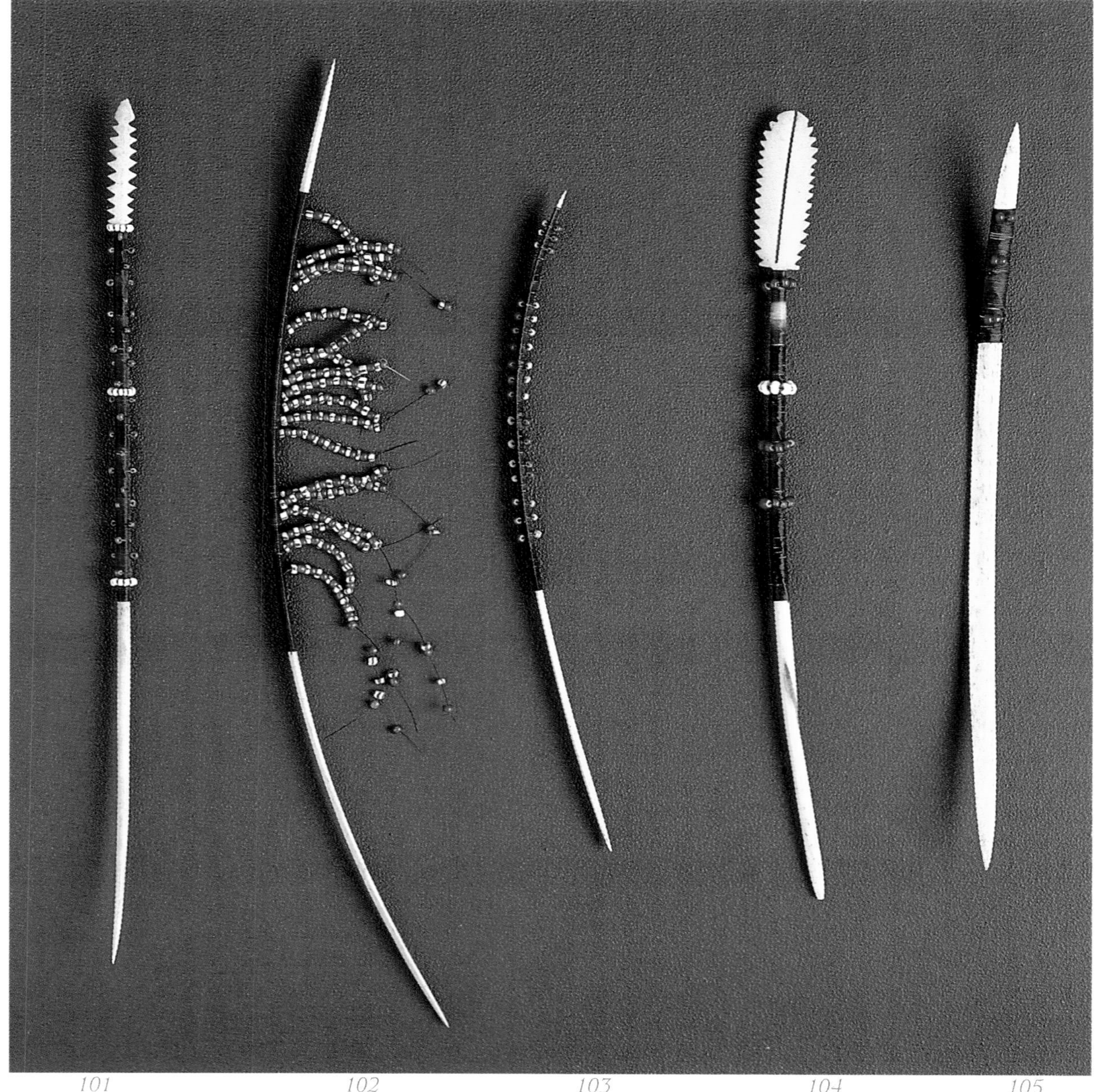

101 102 103 104 105

left:

Nguni
Bone hairpins decorated with hair and beads
late 19th century

101. *length: 25cm*

102. *length: 28.5cm*

103. *length: 19cm*

104. *length: 23cm*

105. *length: 21.5cm*

right:
clockwise

North Nguni
late 19th century

106. Two-part four-strand bracelet
length: 30cm

107. Bracelet
length: 35cm
cf. *Art and ambiguity*, Johannesburg, 1991, p. 116, fig. 100.

108. Six-part twelve-strand strung piece, probably a headband
length: 48 x 3.5cm

109. Probably a necklace
length: 54cm

110. Bracelet
length: 28cm

106 107

110 109 108

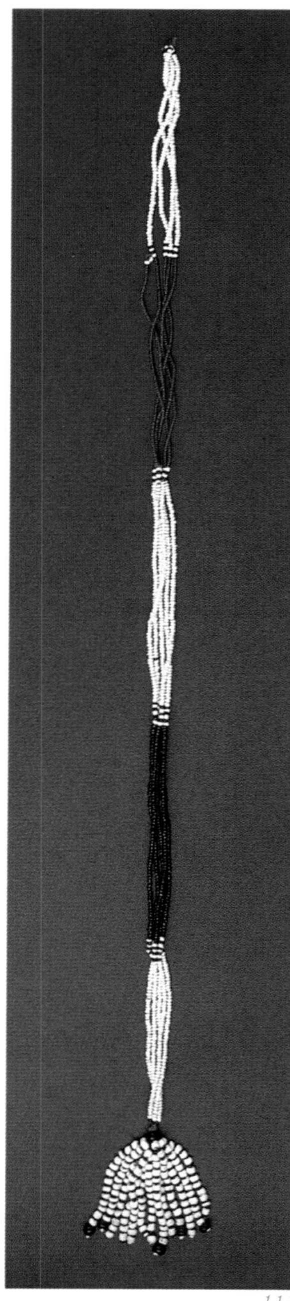

111

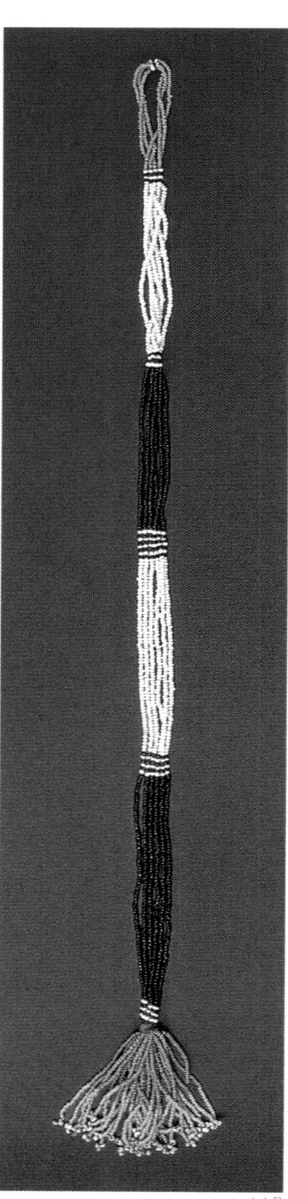

112

left:
Probably Mpondo
Fertility figure pendants
early 20th century

111. *length: 83cm*

112. *length: 73cm*

right:
from left to right
North Nguni
Waistbands or necklaces with fringed section
late 19th century

cf. *Zulu treasures*, Durban, 1996, B45.

113. *80 x 2cm*

114. *73 x 4.5cm*

115. *64 x 3cm*

116. *72 x 5cm*

117. *84 x 5cm*

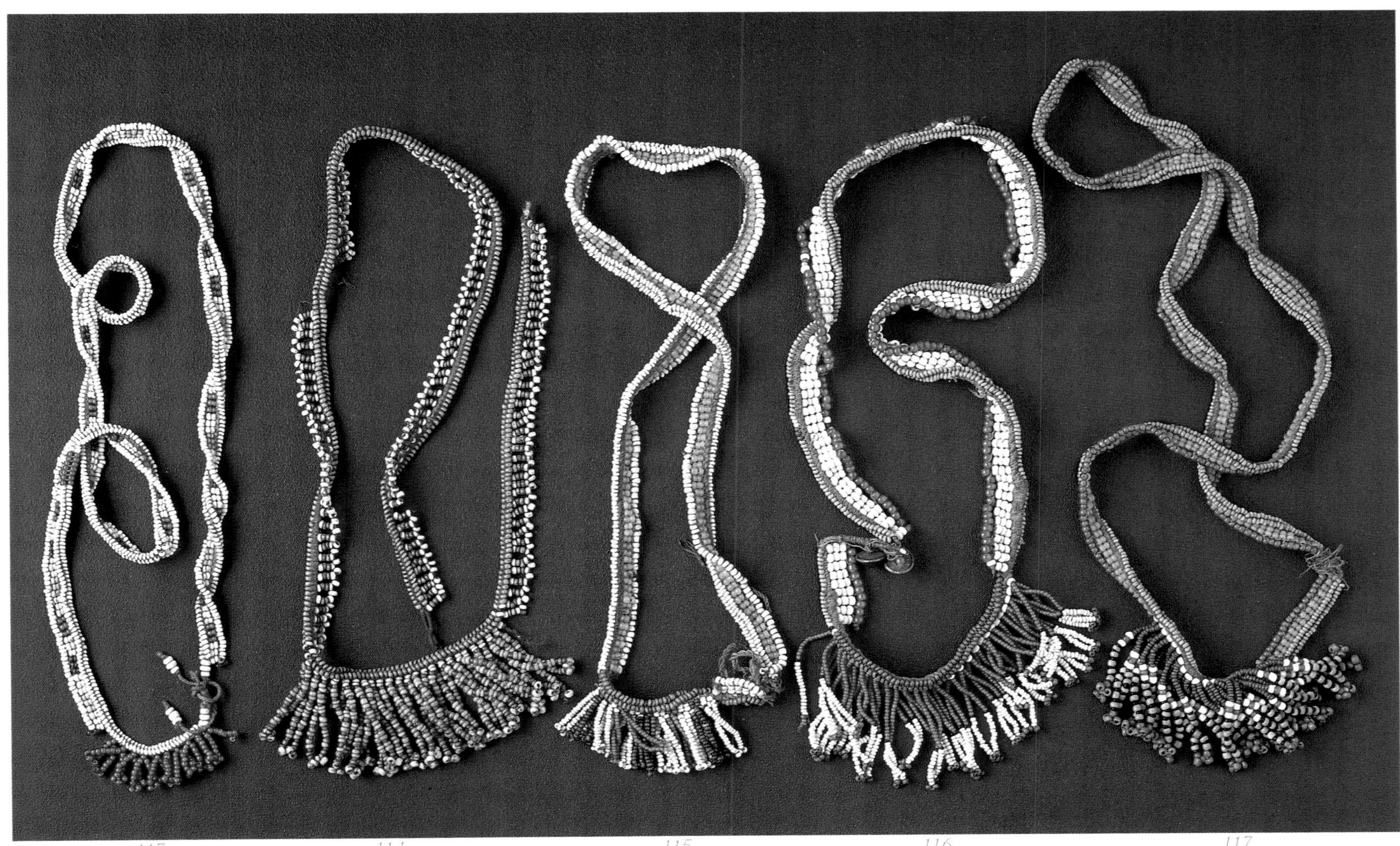

113 114 115 116 117

detail, no. 119

Swazi
Horsehair and bead fertility figures
late 19th century

left:
detail, no. 119

right:
118. *overall length: 73cm*

Illustrated in *Evocations of the child: fertility figures of the southern African region*, Cape Town, 1998, p. 166, fig. 3.

119. *overall length: 75cm*

cf. *Evocations of the child: fertility figures of the southern African region*, Cape Town, 1998, pp. 166 – 167.

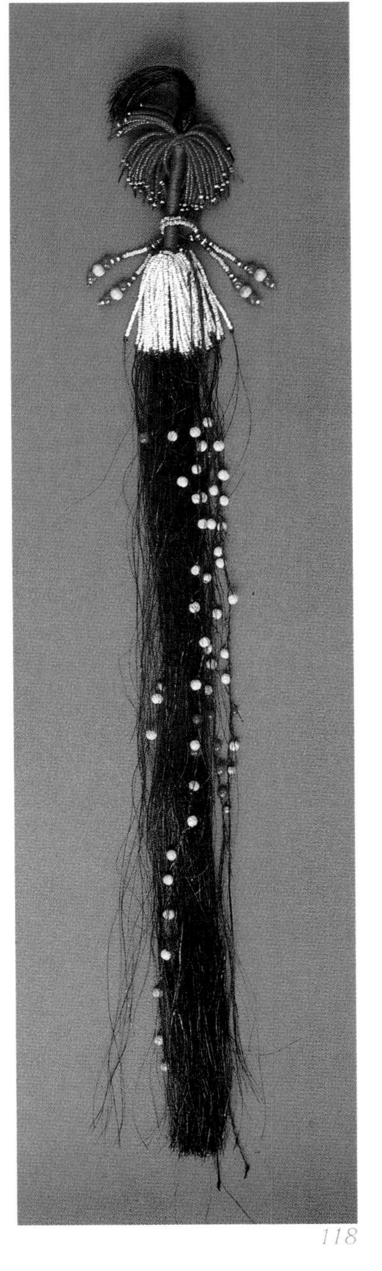

118

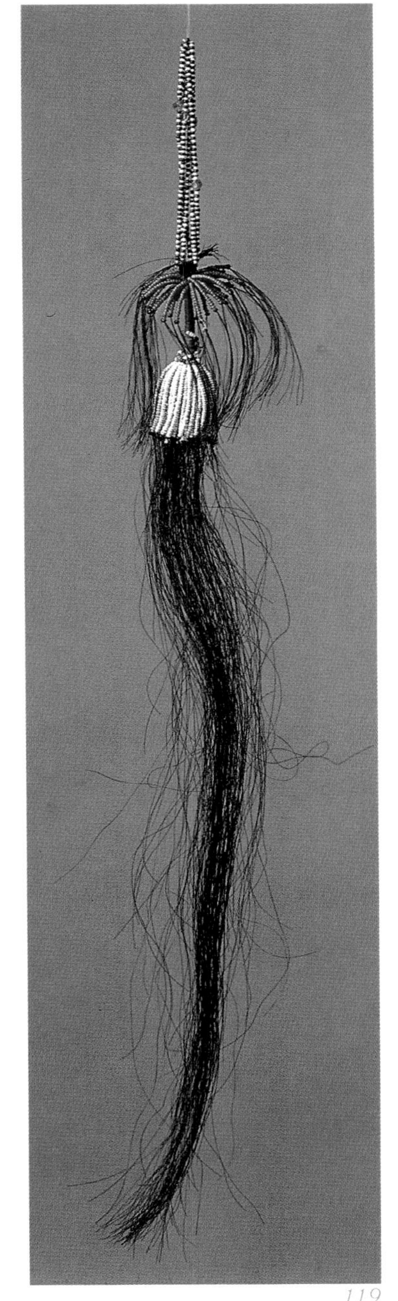

119

120

North Nguni
Beaded cloth skirts
late 19th century

left:
120. *diameter laid out: 54cm (approximately)*

right:
121. *diameter laid out: 42cm*

121

North Nguni
Rolled neckbands
late 19th century

cf. B.V. Brottem and A. Lang, 'Zulu beadwork', *African arts*, Spring 1973, 6(3), p. 9; *Zulu treasures*, Durban, 1996, B11–B19.

left:
detail of the *umbijo* technique

right:
top to bottom
122. *length: 36cm*

123. *length: 36cm*

124. *length: 42cm*

125. *length: 44cm*

126. *length: 48cm*

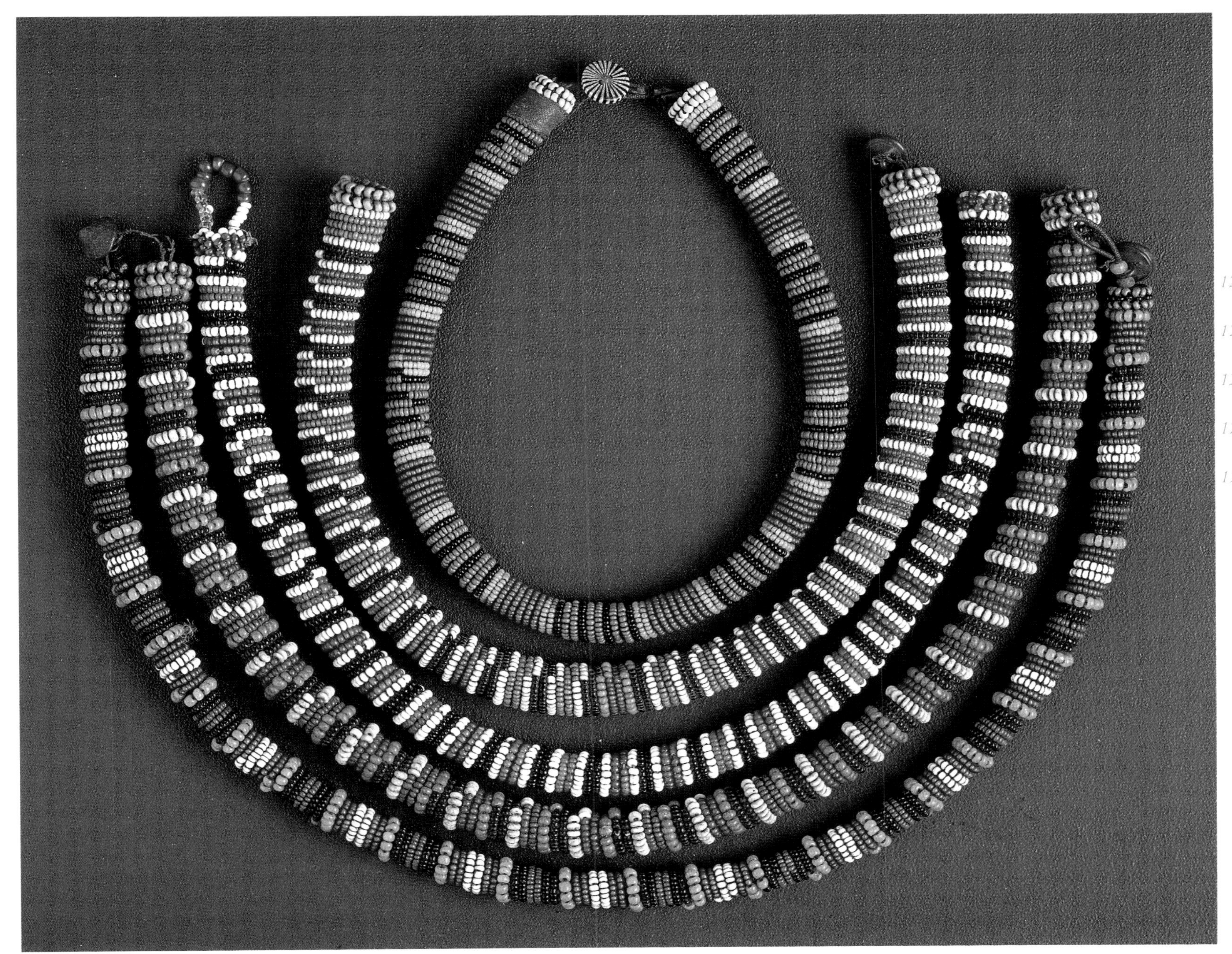

122

123

124

125

126

127

left:
127. North Nguni
Neckpiece
late 19th century
panel: 8.5 x 10cm, length of roll: 40cm
cf. *Art and ambiguity*, Johannesburg, 1991, p. 8, pl. 8.

North Nguni
Rolled neckbands or waistbands
late 19th century

right:
top to bottom
128. *length: 36cm*
129. *length: 50cm*
130. *length: 54cm*
131. *length: 60cm*
132. *length: 65cm*
133. *length: 77cm*
134. *length: 81cm*
135. *length: 85cm*

following page:
left:
top to bottom
136. *length: 36cm*
137. *length: 38cm*
138. *length: 45cm*
139. *length: 48cm*
140. *length: 60cm*

right:
top to bottom
141. *length: 42cm*
142. *length: 47cm*
143. *length: 59cm*
144. *length: 87cm*
145. *length: 88cm*
146. *length: 85cm*

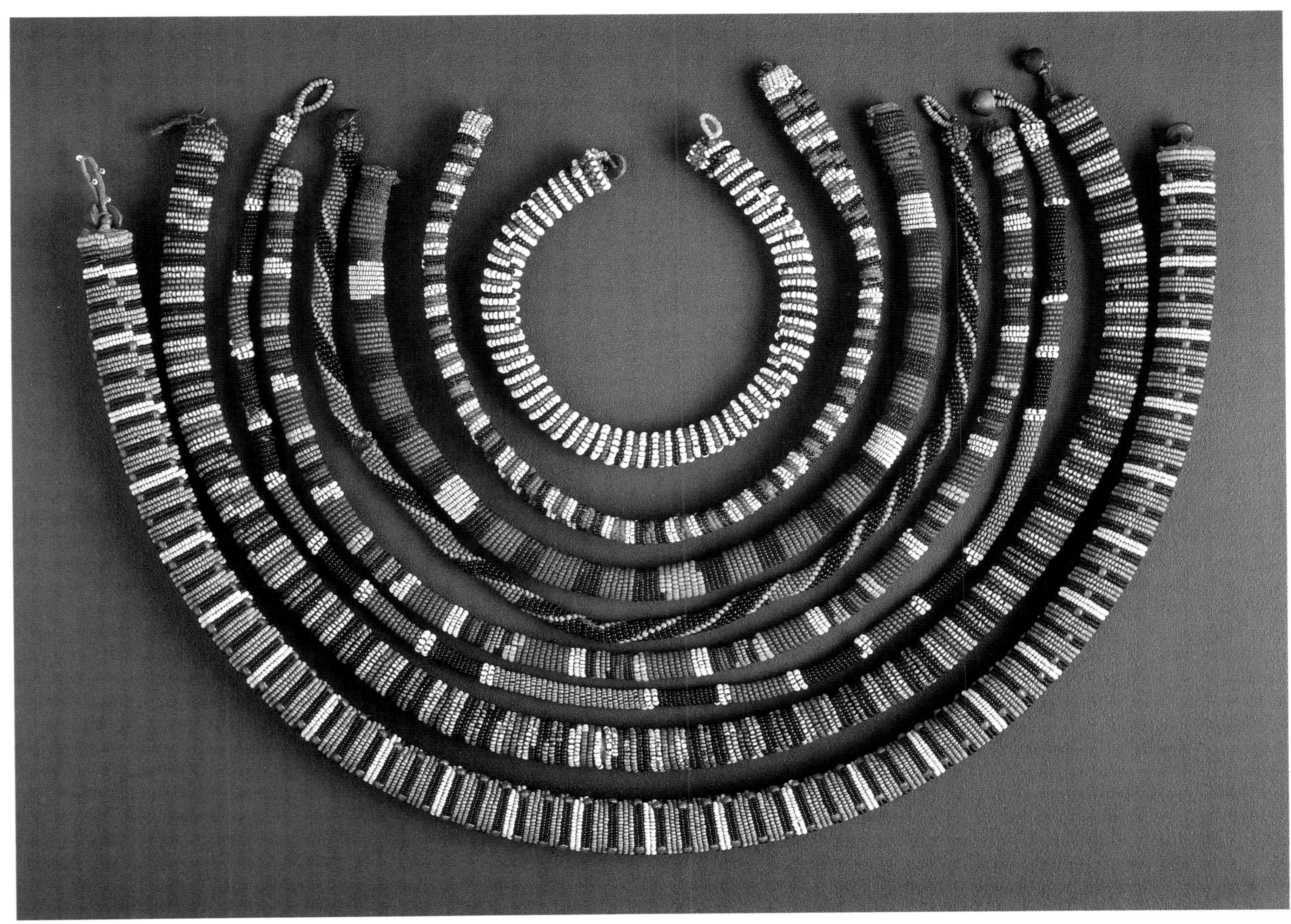

128
129
130
131
132
133
134
135

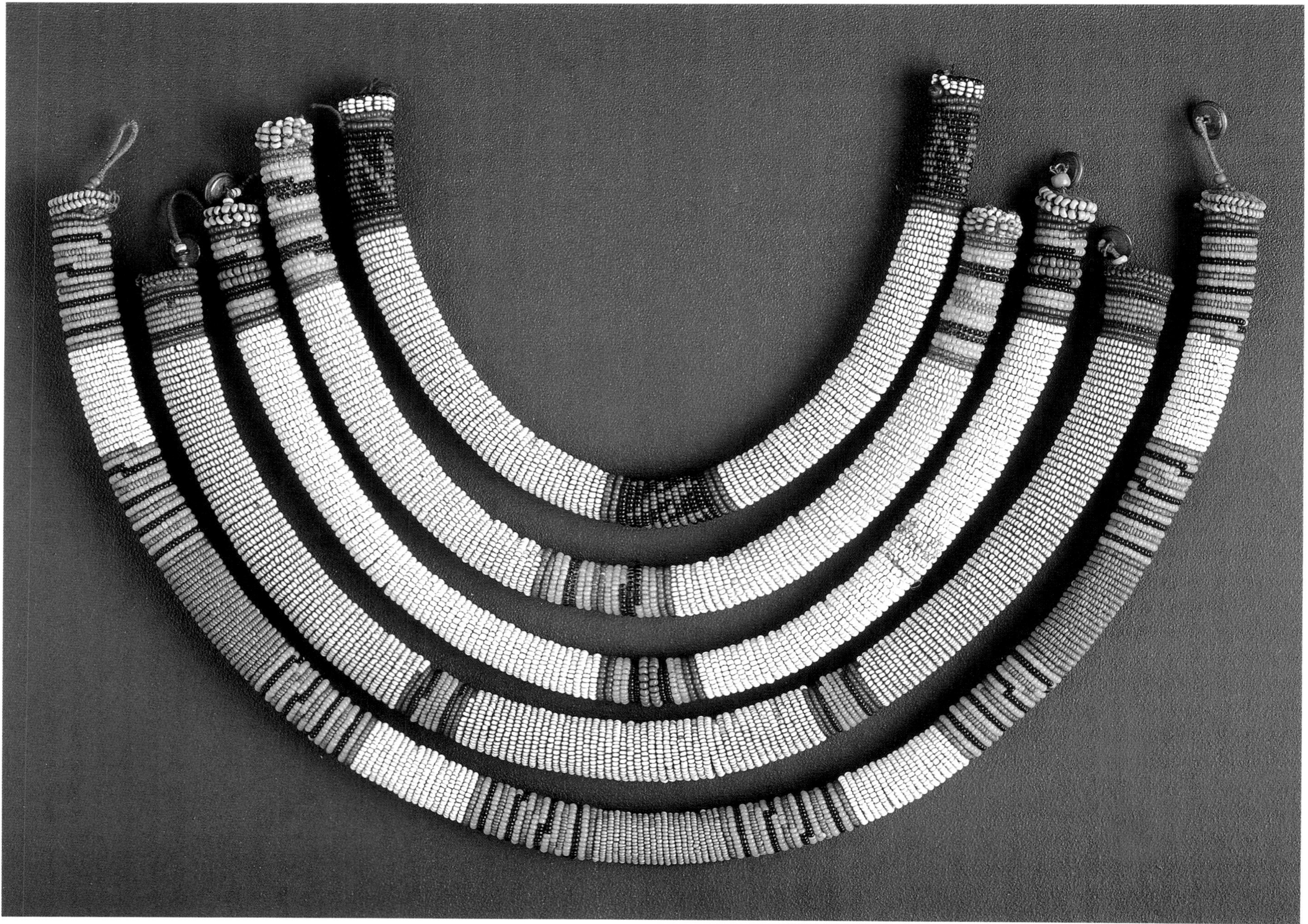

136
137
138
139
140

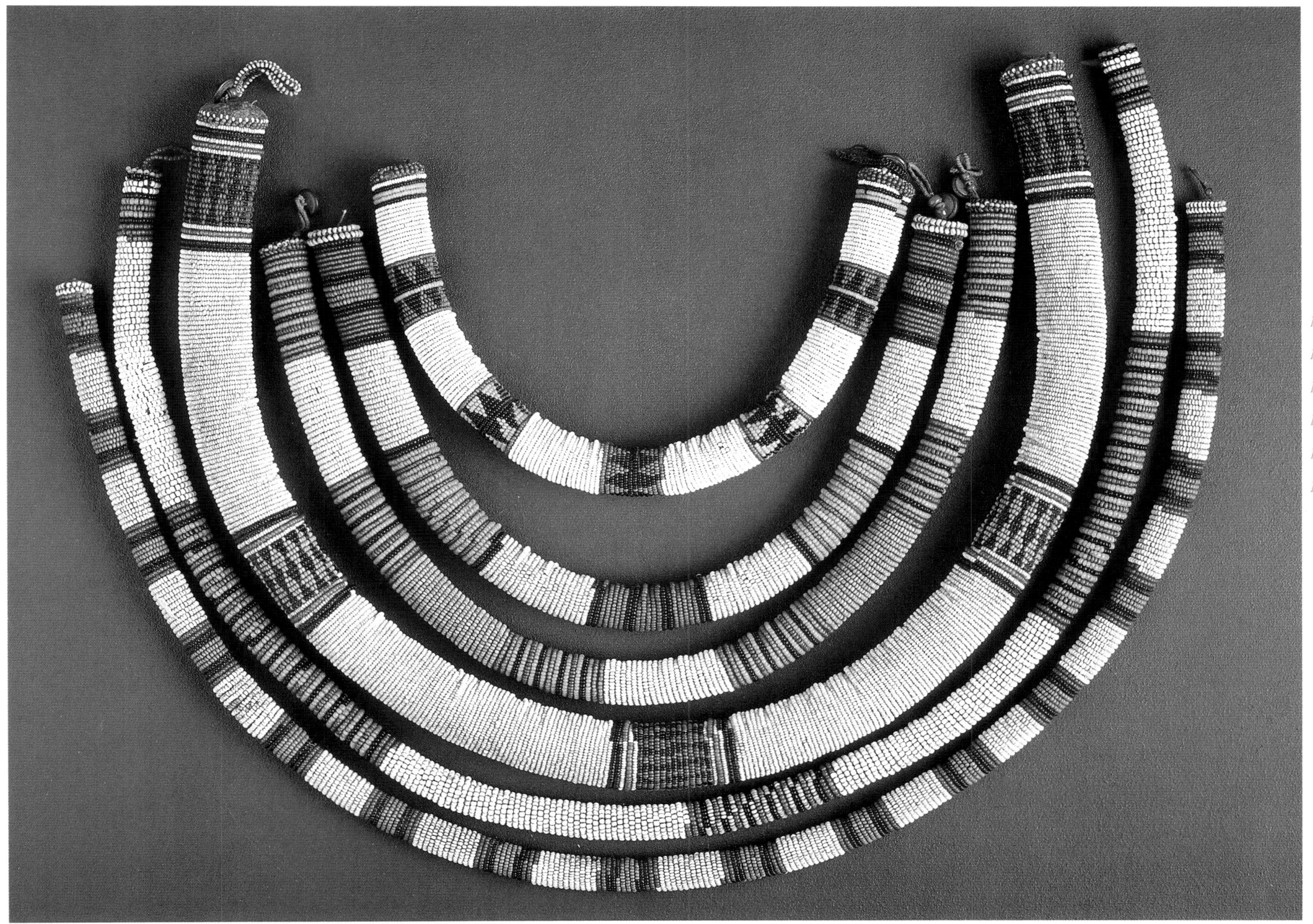

141
142
143
144
145
146

147

North Nguni
late 19th century

left:
147. Five-roll waistband
84 x 5cm

right:
148. Four-roll waistband with tassels
71 x 4cm (excluding tassels)

149. Eight-roll waistband
75 x 8cm

150. Six-roll waistband
73 x 7cm
cf. *Zulu treasures*, Durban, 1996, B64.

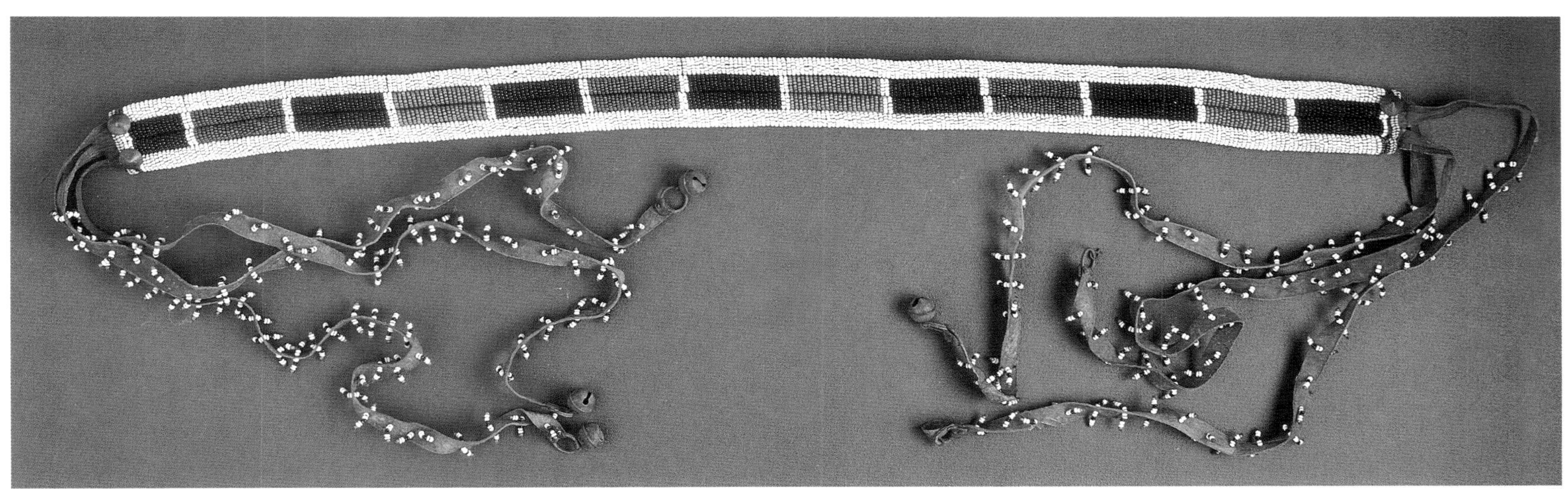

148

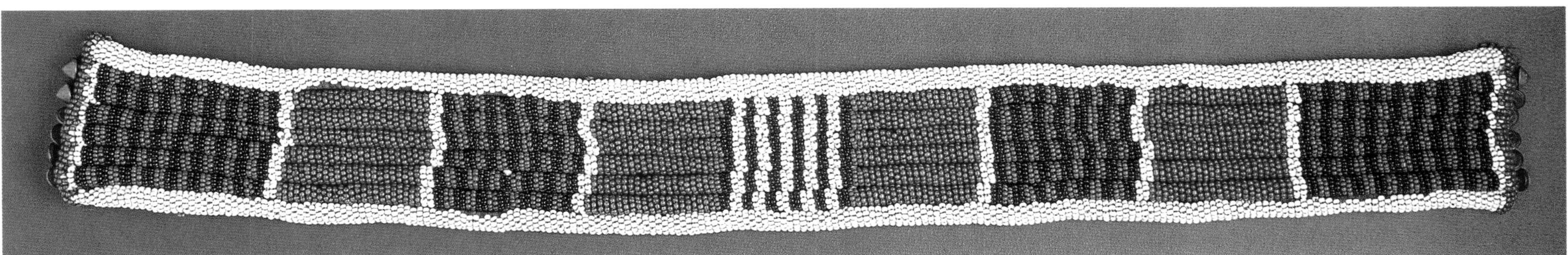

149

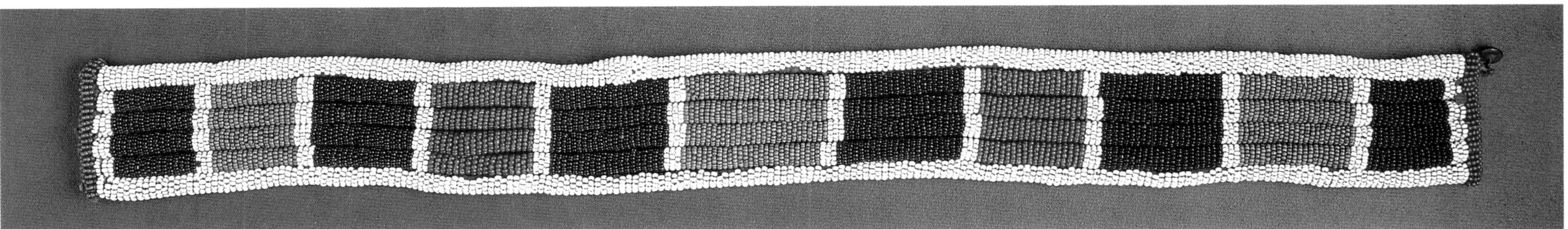

150

detail, reverse of no. 154

North Nguni
late 19th century

left:
detail, reverse of no. 154

right:
151. Ten-roll waistband with apron panel
apron: 6 x 19.5cm, waistband: 93 x 8cm

152. Four-roll waistband
81 x 4.5cm

153. Eight-roll waistband
72 x 7cm

154. Six-roll waistband
68 x 6.5cm

155. Twisted nine-roll waistband
length: 69cm

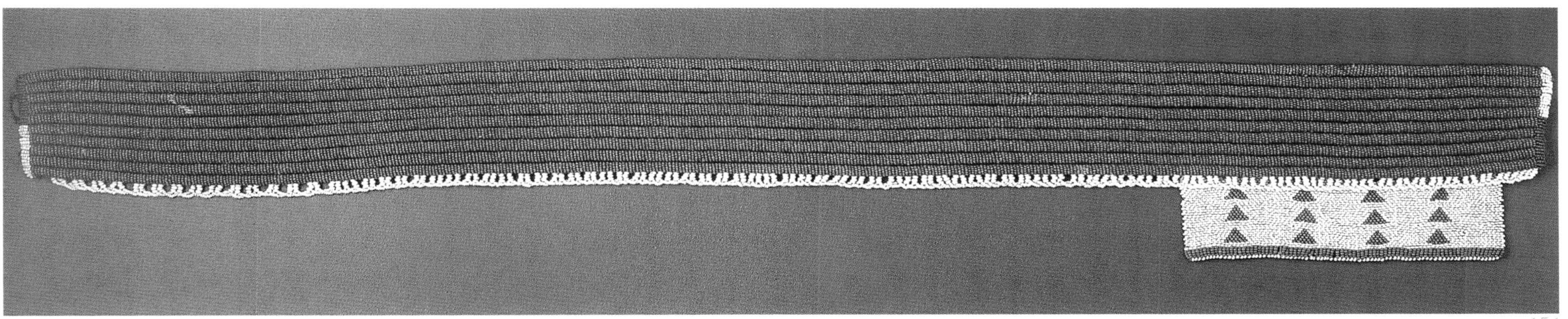

151

152

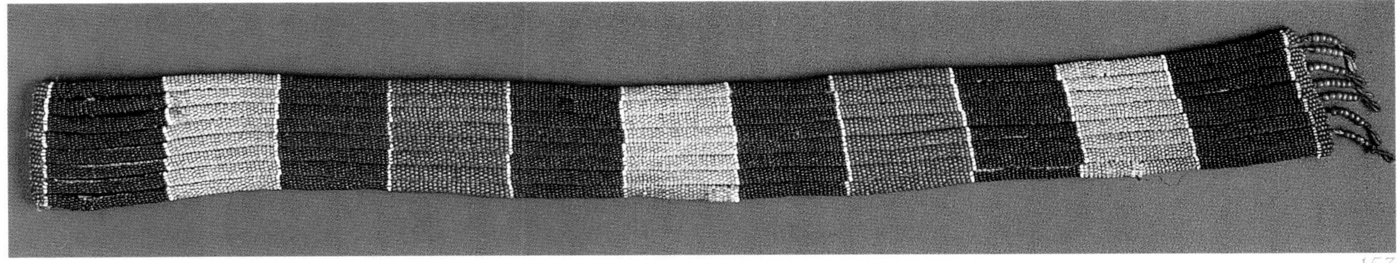

153

154

155

156

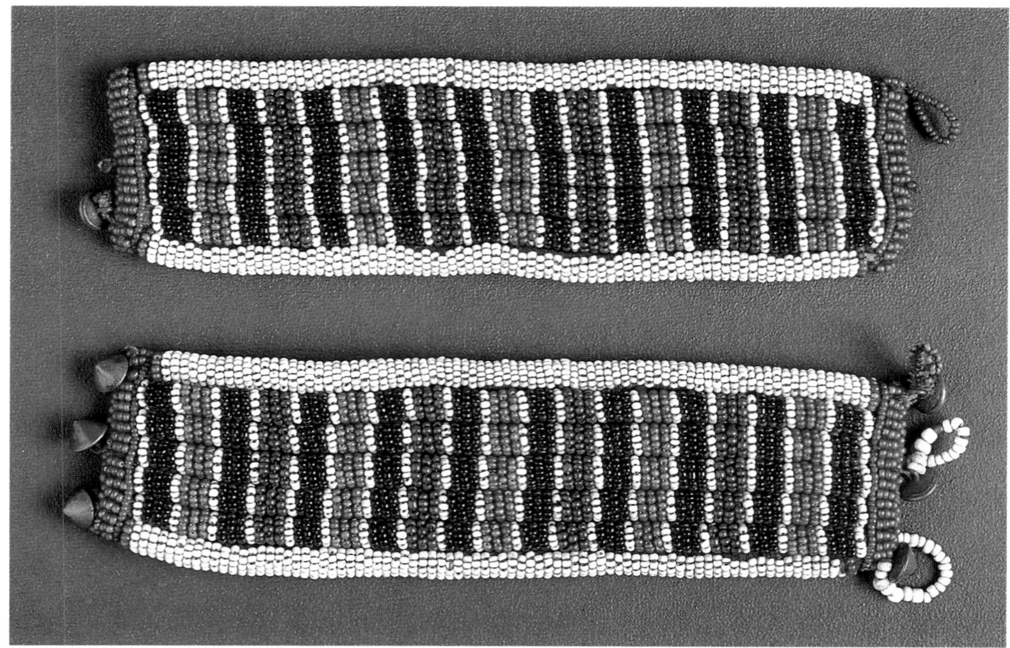

157

North Nguni
late 19th century

left:

156. Pair of eight-roll anklets
6.5 x 19cm each

157. Pair of seven-roll anklets
6 x 23cm each

right:

158. Pair of fourteen-roll anklets
16 x 29cm each

158

159

North Nguni

left:

159. Three-roll waistband with apron panel
late 19th century
panel: 8.5 x 12cm, waistband: 77 x 5cm

right:

160. Two-roll waistband with two apron panels
early 20th century
pink panel: 11.5 x 14cm, blue and white panel: 8.5 x 14.5cm, waistband: 91 x 2cm

161. Six-roll waistband with apron panel
late 19th century
panel: 6.5 x 20cm, waistband: 83 x 8cm (excluding tassels)

160

161

detail, no. 162

North Nguni
late 19th century

left:
detail, no. 162

right:
162. Four-roll waistband with back and front aprons
bead panel: 8 x 12cm, leather panel: 20 x 16cm, waistband: 84 x 5.5cm

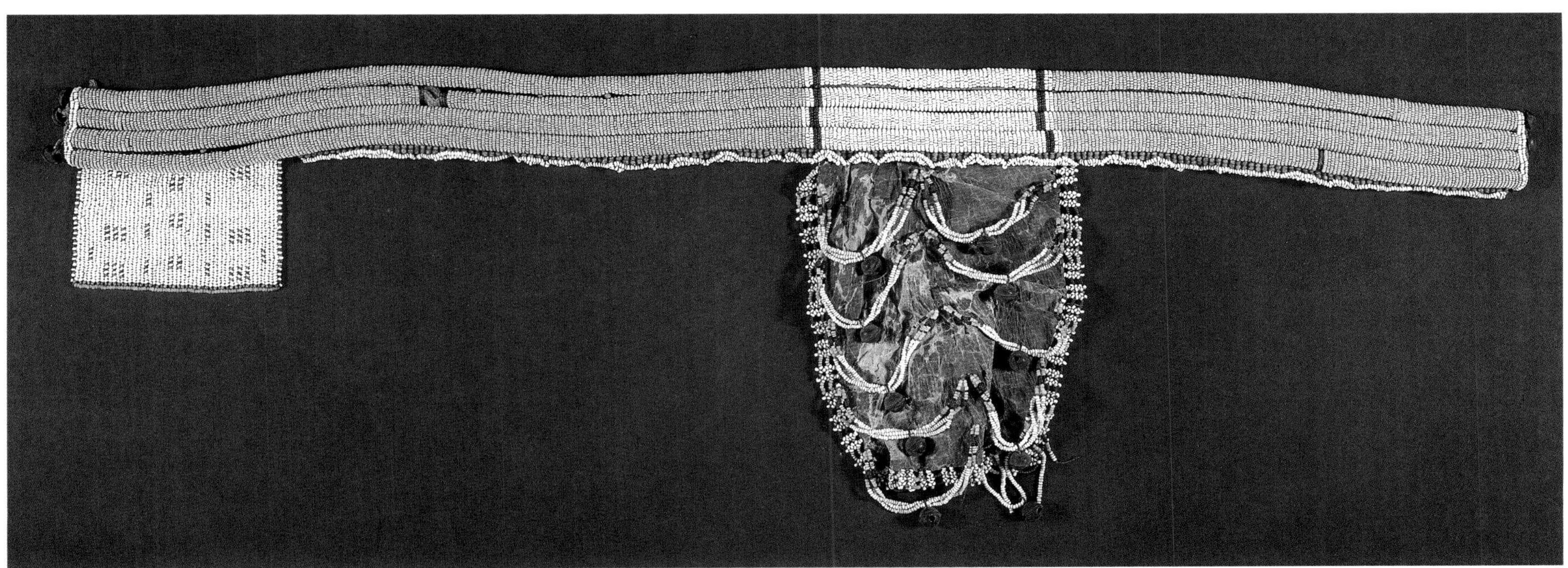

162

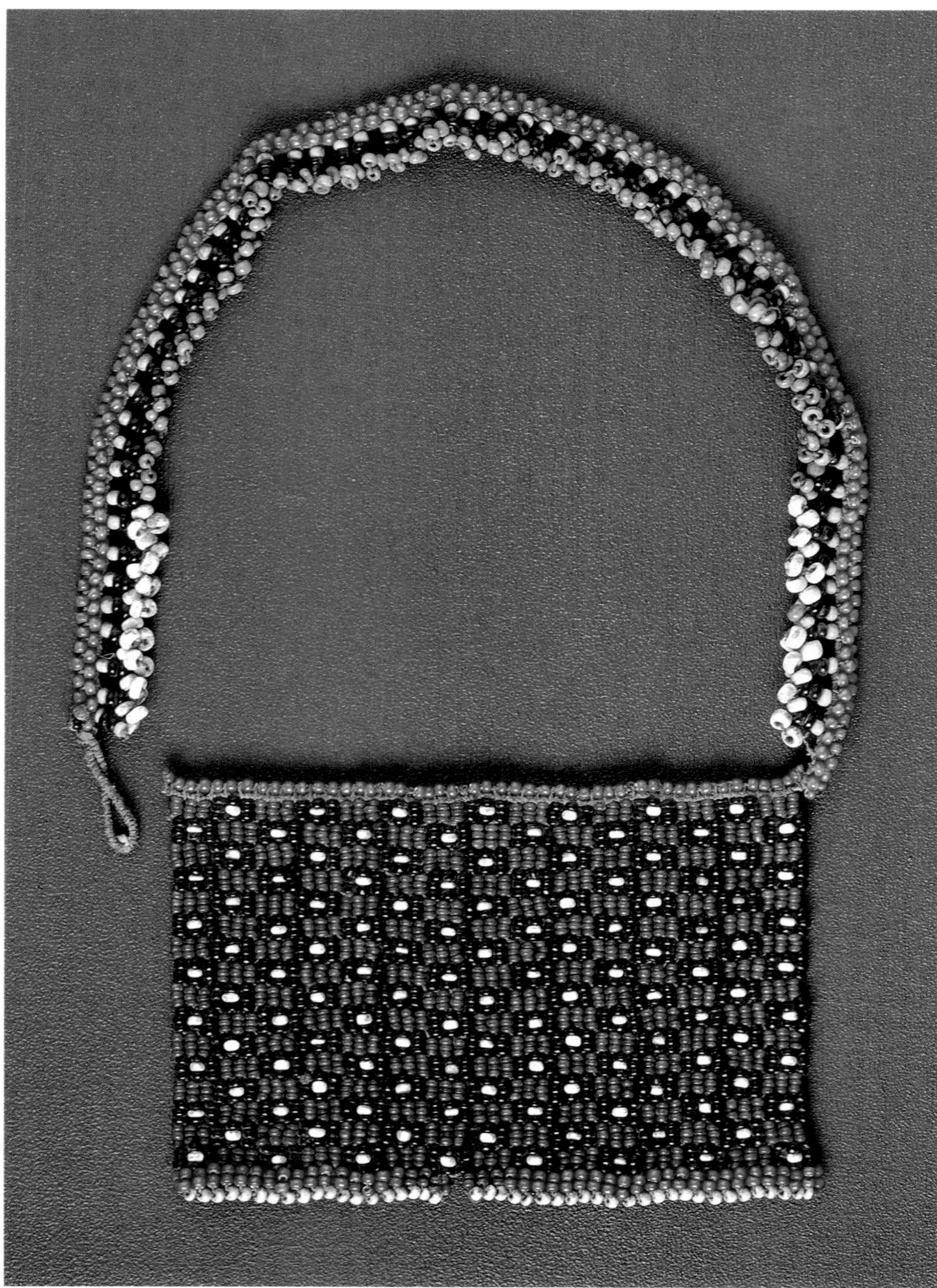

163

North Nguni
late 19th century

left:
163. Neckpiece
panel: 9 x 13.5cm

right:
164. Two-roll waistband with a fringed apron
apron: 15 x 22cm, overall length: 81cm

165. Three-roll waistband with fringe
80 x 15cm

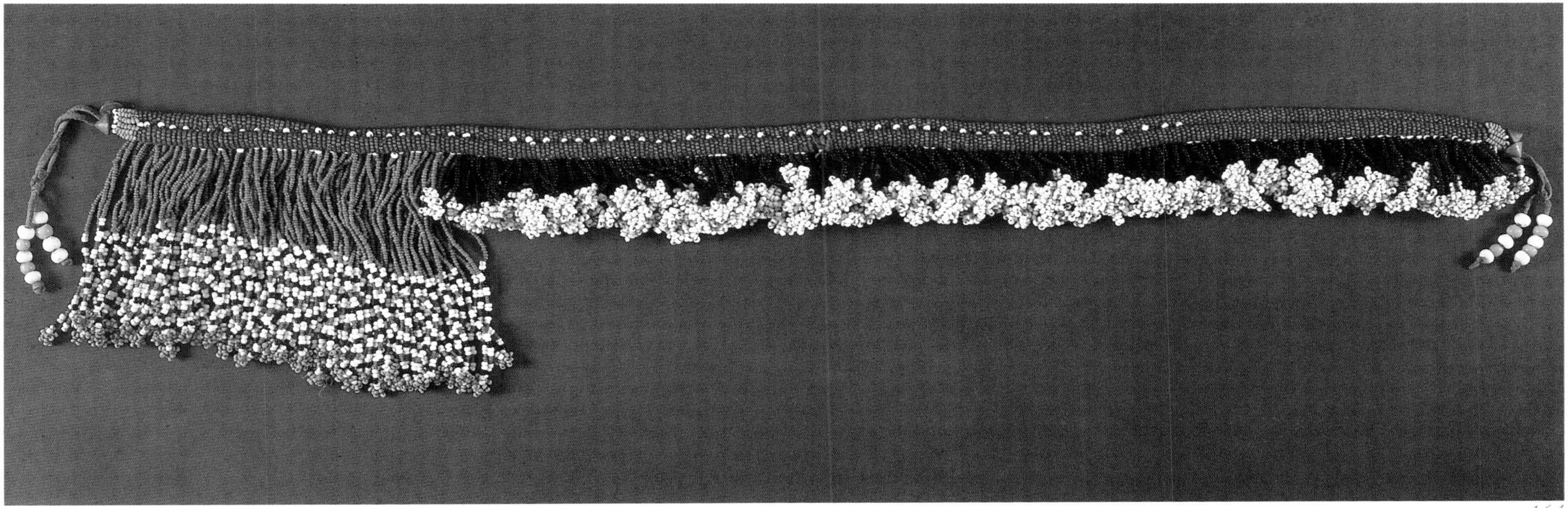

164

165

detail, no. 166

North Nguni
Married women's beaded grass waistbands
late 19th century

left:
detail, no. 166

right:
166. *62 x 4cm (excluding straps)*

167. *76 x 6cm (excluding straps)*

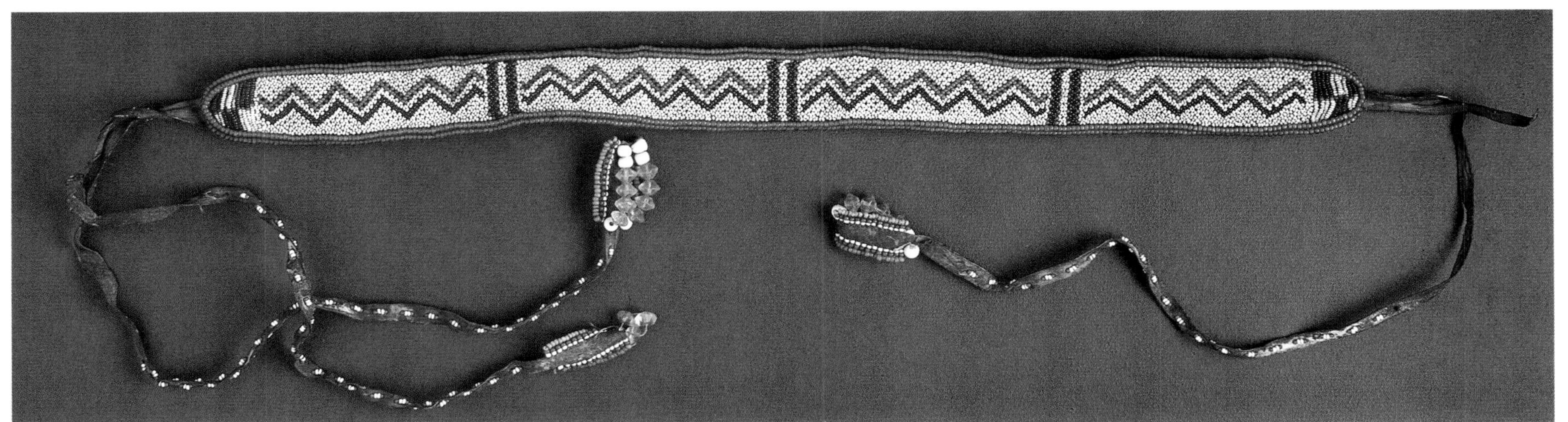

166

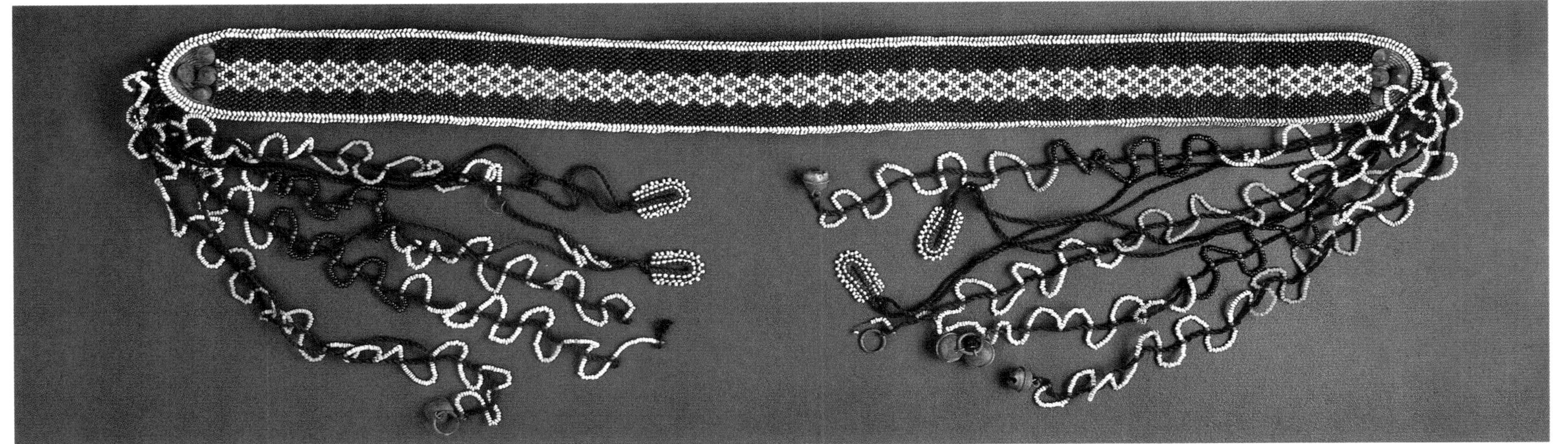

167

168

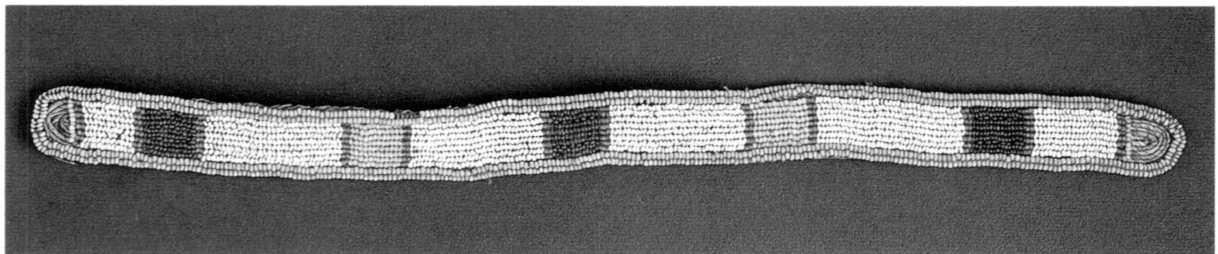
169

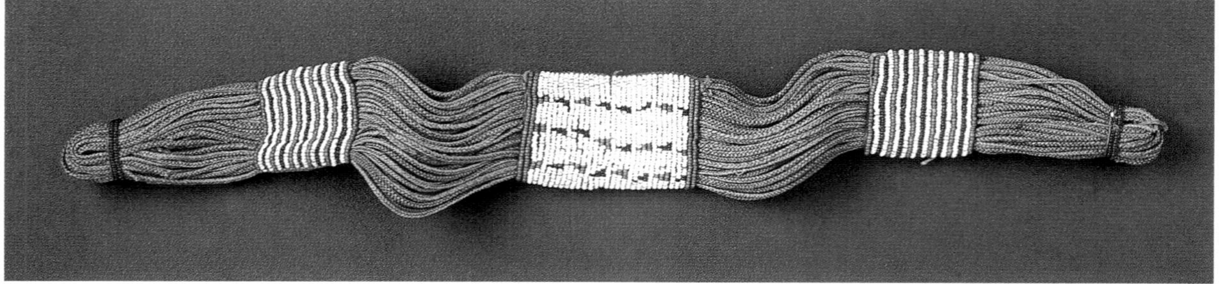
170

North Nguni
Married women's beaded grass waistbands
late 19th century

left:
168. *56 x 6cm*

169. *46 x 3cm*

170. *52 x 6cm*

right:
171. *62 x 5.5cm*

172. *68 x 7cm*
cf. the design to *Art and ambiguity*, Johannesburg, 1991, cat. no. 745.

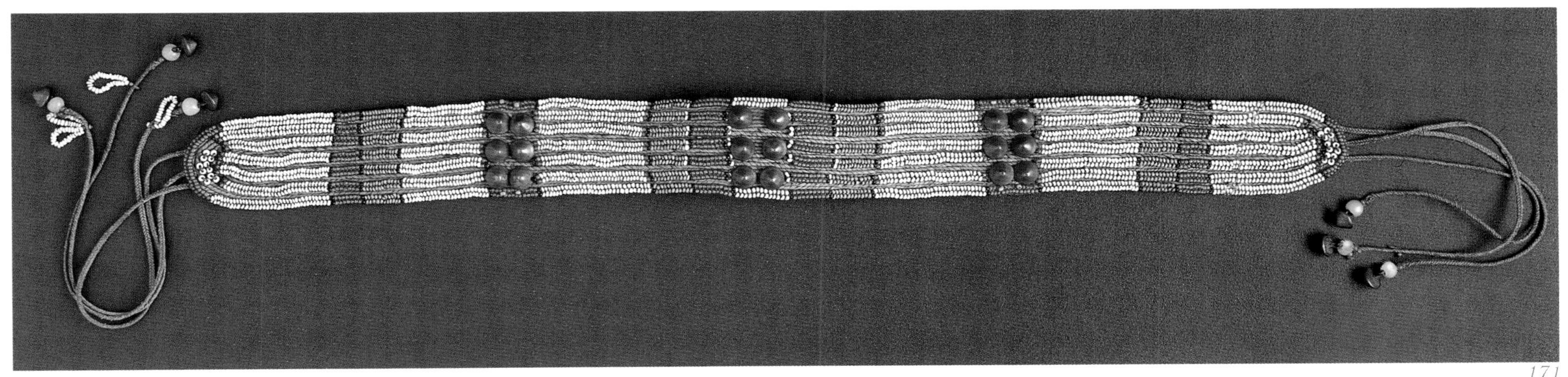

171

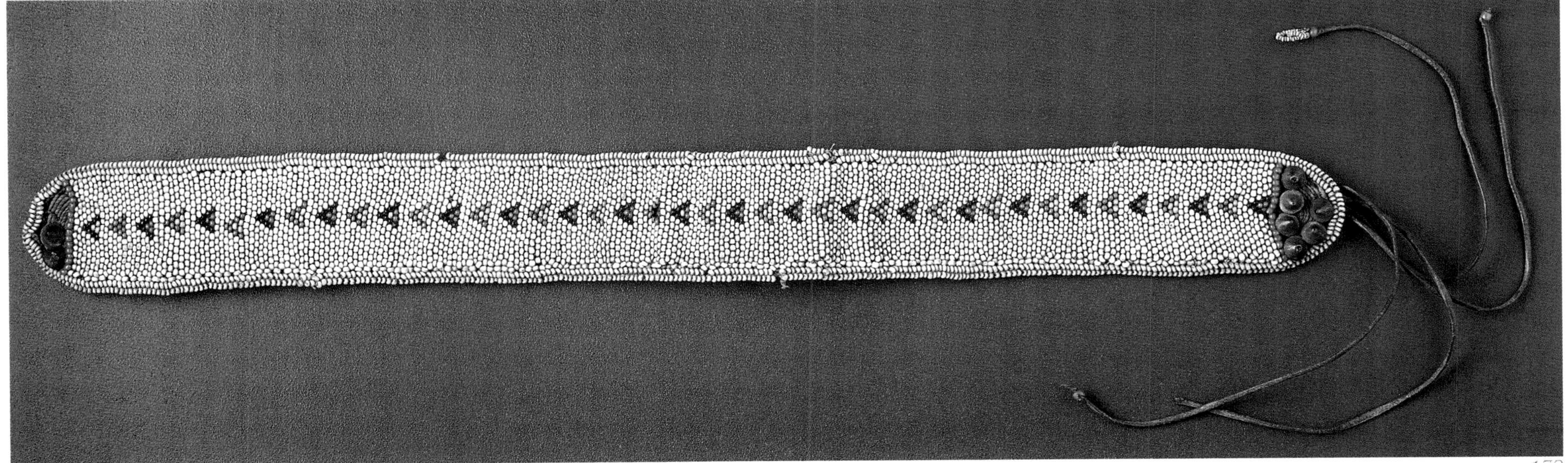

172

173

North Nguni
Neckpieces
late 19th century

left:
173. *panel: 12.5 x 11cm*

right:
174. *panel: 16 x 12cm*

175. *panel: 24 x 12.5cm*

174

175

176

North Nguni
Neckpieces
late 19th century

left:
176. *central panel: 29 x 17cm*

right:
177. *central panel: 25 x 10.5cm*

178. *central panel: 26 x 10cm*

177

178

179

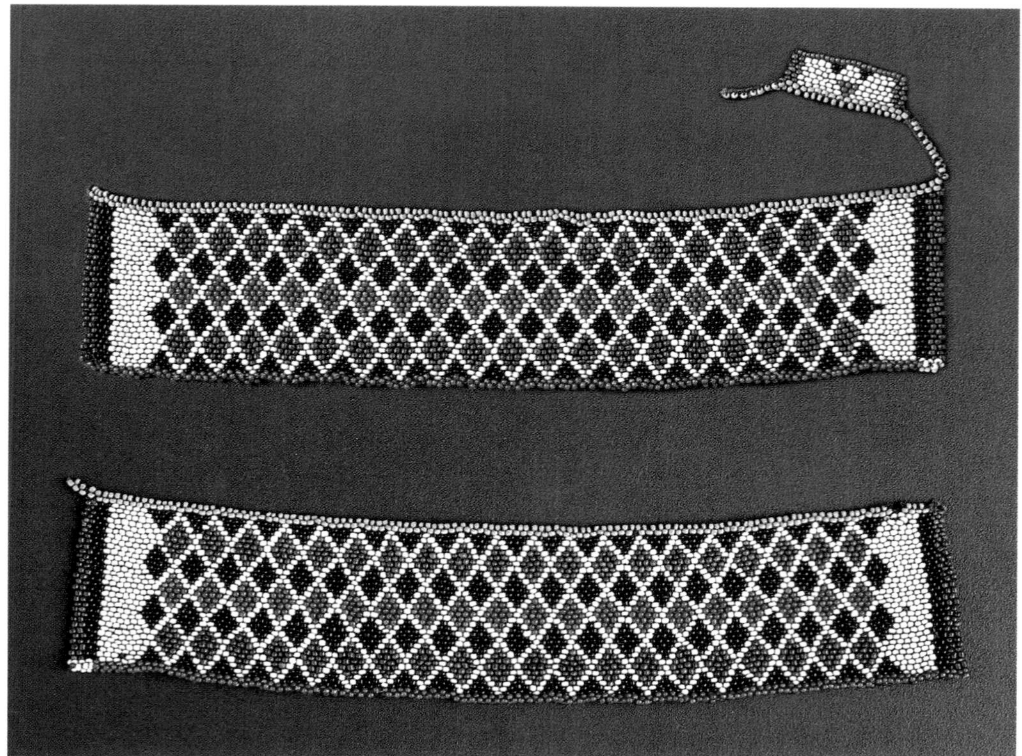

180

North Nguni
late 19th century

left:
179. Pair of panels
6.5 x 24cm each

180. Pair of panels
8 x 39cm each
cf. *Zulu treasures*, B29.

right:
181. Bandolier
96 x 4.5cm
cf. *Zulu treasures*, Durban, 1996, B29; *Art and ambiguity*, Johannesburg, 1991, cat. no. 735.

181

182

North Nguni
late 19th century

left:
182. Bandolier
each panel: 104 x 5.5cm
cf. B.V. Brottem and A. Lang, 'Zulu beadwork', *African arts*, Spring 1973, 6(3), p. 12.

right:
183. Waistband or bandolier
main panel: 87 x 8cm

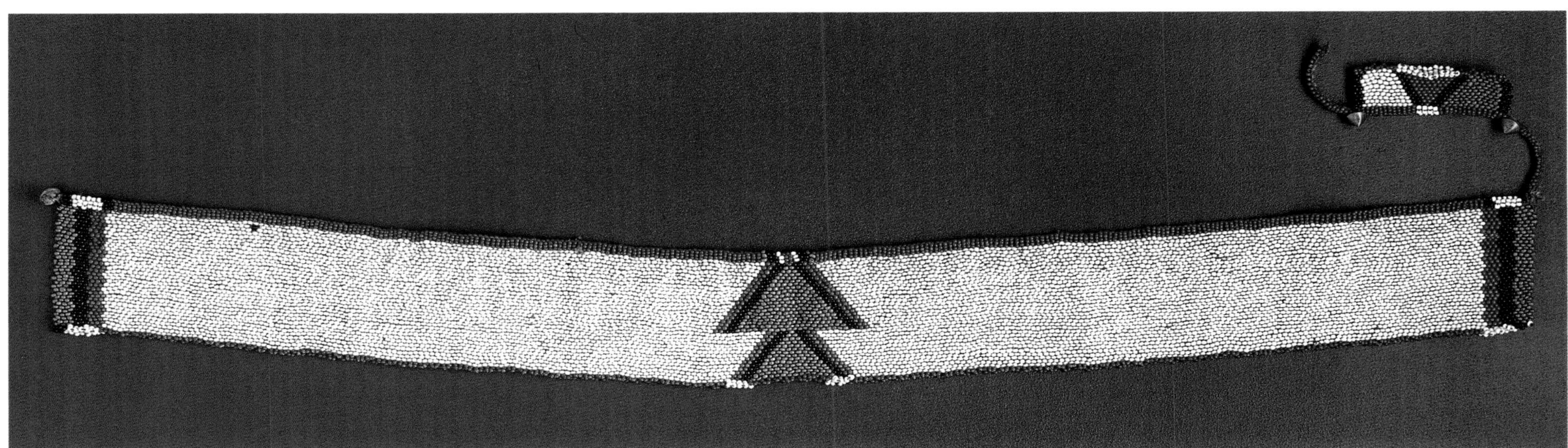

183

184

North Nguni
Neckpieces or waistbands
late 19th century

left:

184. *two main panels: 33 x 5.5cm each, small central panel: 17 x 6cm*

right:

185. *two main panels: 27 x 6cm each, small central panel: 13 x 6cm*

186. *two main panels: 37 x 8cm each, small central panel: 13 x 3.5cm*

185

186

detail, no. 187

left:
detail, no. 187

right:
187. North Nguni
Circular shoulder piece
late 19th century
length: 156 x 5cm, diameter: 60cm

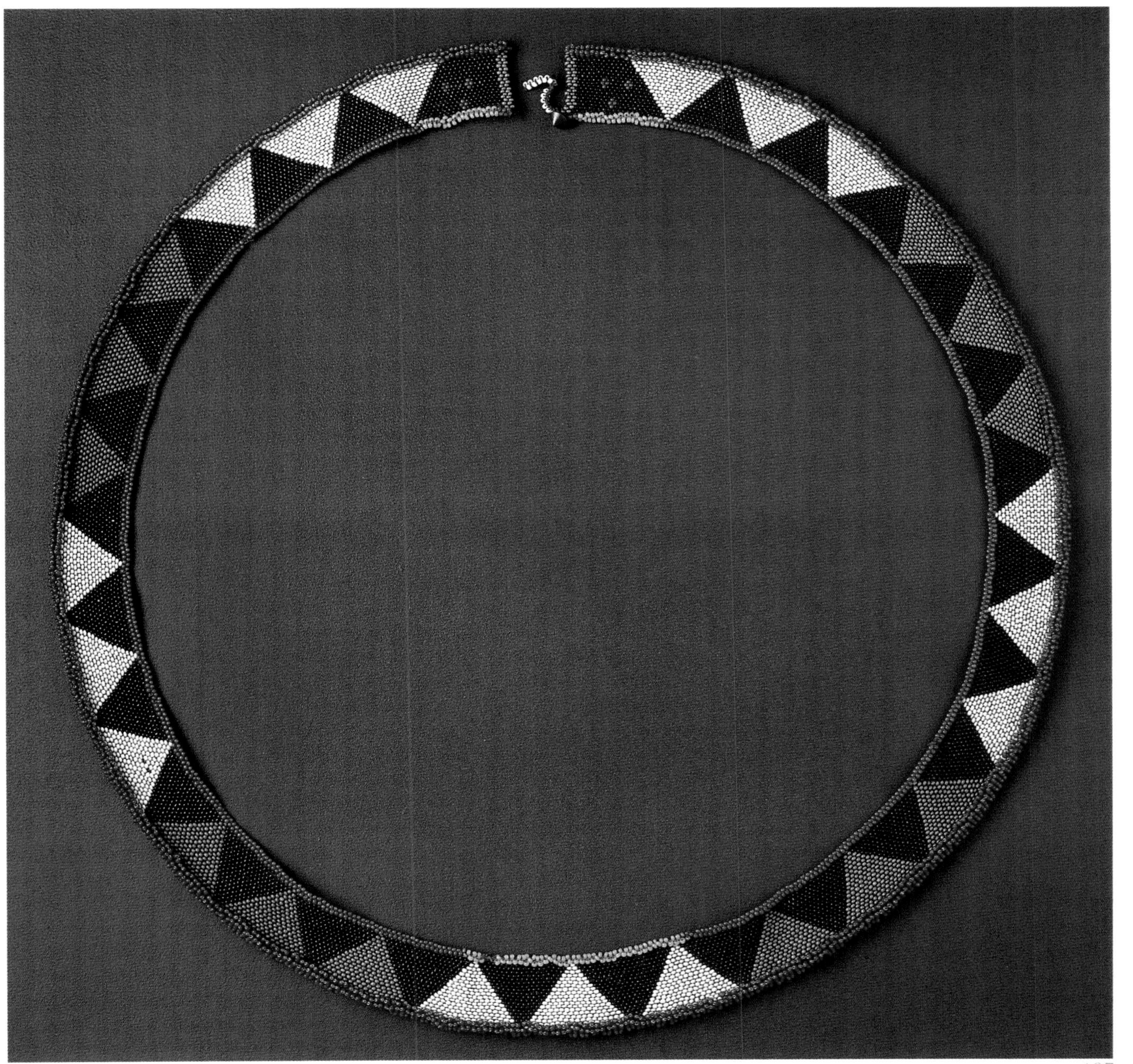

187

188

189

190

North Nguni
late 19th century

left:
188. Neckpiece
panel: 15 x 8cm

189. Panel
14 x 15.5cm

190. Pouch
10.5 x 10cm

right:
191. Neckpiece
panel: 9.5 x 11cm

192. Neckpiece with pouch
pouch: 9.5 x 10cm

193. Neckpiece
panel: 10.5 x 10cm

191

192

193

194

North Nguni
late 19th century

left:
194. Waistband with apron panel
panel: 13 x 21cm, length of waistband: 54cm

right:
Neckpieces
Nos. 195 and 196 have the attached note: 'Zulu bead ornaments, etc. Brought home by my brother Elliott after wintering in South Africa, on account of failing health ... F.E. Walsh. One or two of the Bead Ornaments added by A.C.W. – sent to her by Kathleen Donald from South Africa. Elliott Crompton died 1895' written on a card of 'Mrs Leo Walsh, Larchwood, Chelford'

195. *panel: 13.5 x 7cm*

196. *panel: 10 x 6cm*

197. Neckpiece
pouch: 9 x 10.5cm

following two pages:
left:
Neckpieces

198. *62 x 6.5cm (laid out straight)*

199. *large panel: 30 x 9.5cm, small panels: 8 x 5cm each*

right:
200. Two-roll fringed waistband with apron panel
panel: 9.5 x 15cm, waistband: 73 x 5cm

201. Neckpiece
panel: 10 x 15.5cm

202. Neckpiece
panel: 9 x 6.5cm

203. Panel
17 x 9cm

195

196

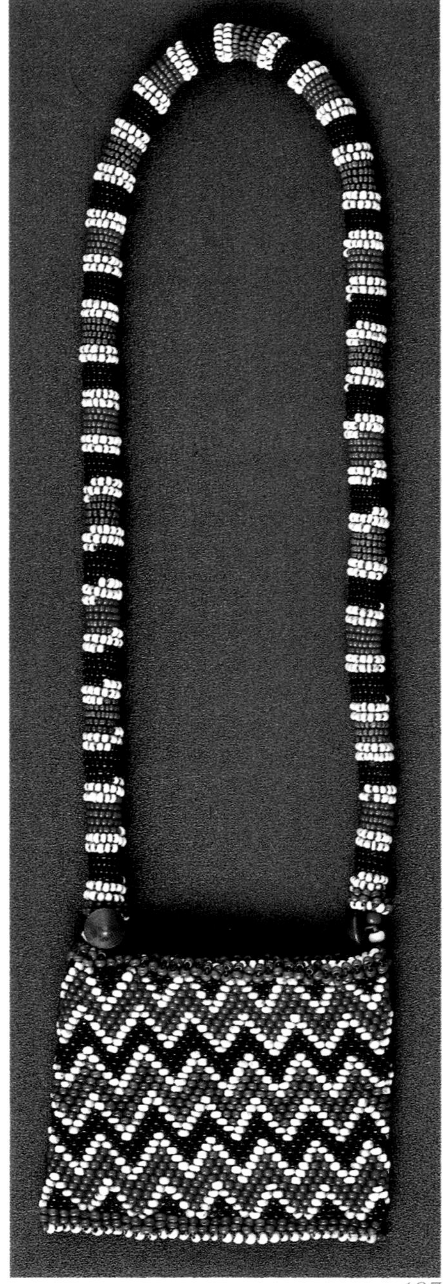
197

198

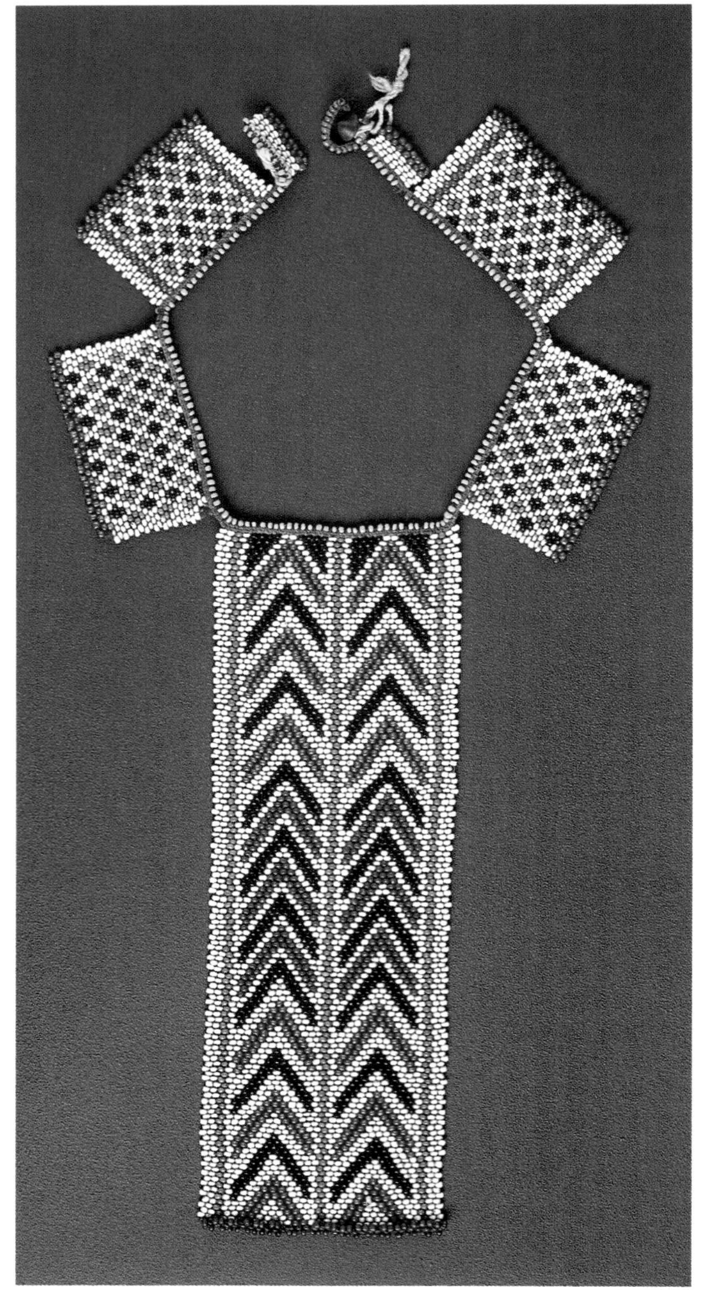

199

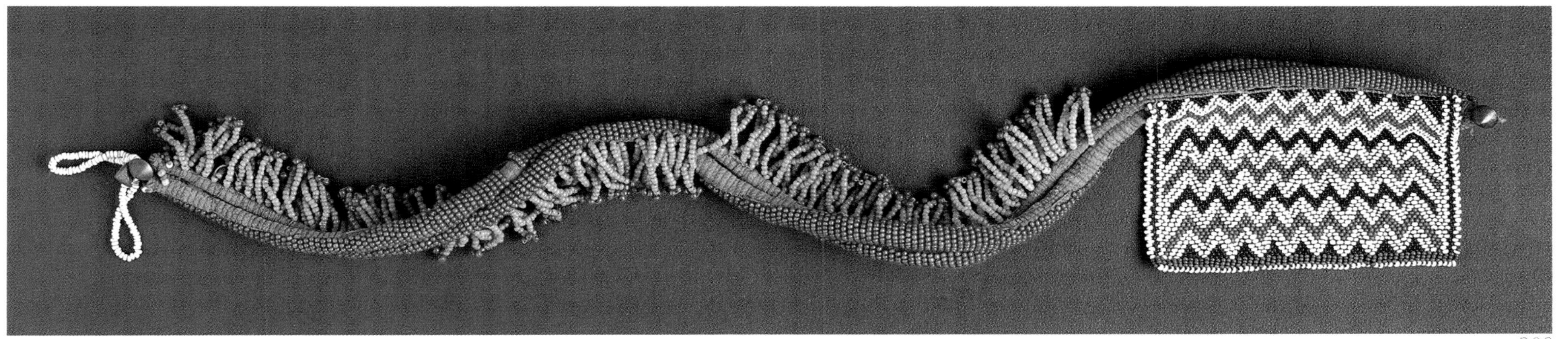

200

201

202

203

204

205

North Nguni
late 19th century

left:
Pouches

204. *8 x 7.5cm*

205. *8.5 x 8cm*

right:
206. Apron panel
16 x 26cm
cf. *Evocations of the child: fertility figures of the southern African region*, Cape Town, 1998, p. 158.

following page:
Waistbands with apron panel

left:
207. *panel: 18.5 x 14cm, length of waistband: 65cm*

right:
208. *panel: 11.5 x 19cm, length of waistband: 64cm*

206

207

208

209

North Nguni
late 19th century

left:
209. Apron panel
10 x 29cm

cf. *Art and ambiguity*, Johannesburg, 1991, cat. no. 693; *Zulu treasures*, Durban, 1996, B24.

right:
210. Shaped waistband with apron panel
overall length: 77cm, apron panel: 8.5 x 20cm

cf. a similar waistband and apron in Local History Museum, Durban, illustrated in *Know the past: wear the future*, Local History Museum Education pamphlet no. 1, 1989, p. 11; and *Zulu treasures*, Durban, 1996, B24.

211. Waistband or bandolier
76 x 4cm

Provenance for the above three pieces: Alfred John Gregory (1851–1927), who lived at the Cape between 1891 and 1914 and served as Medical Officer of Health for the Cape Colony between 1901 and 1910. See DSAB, vol. 5.

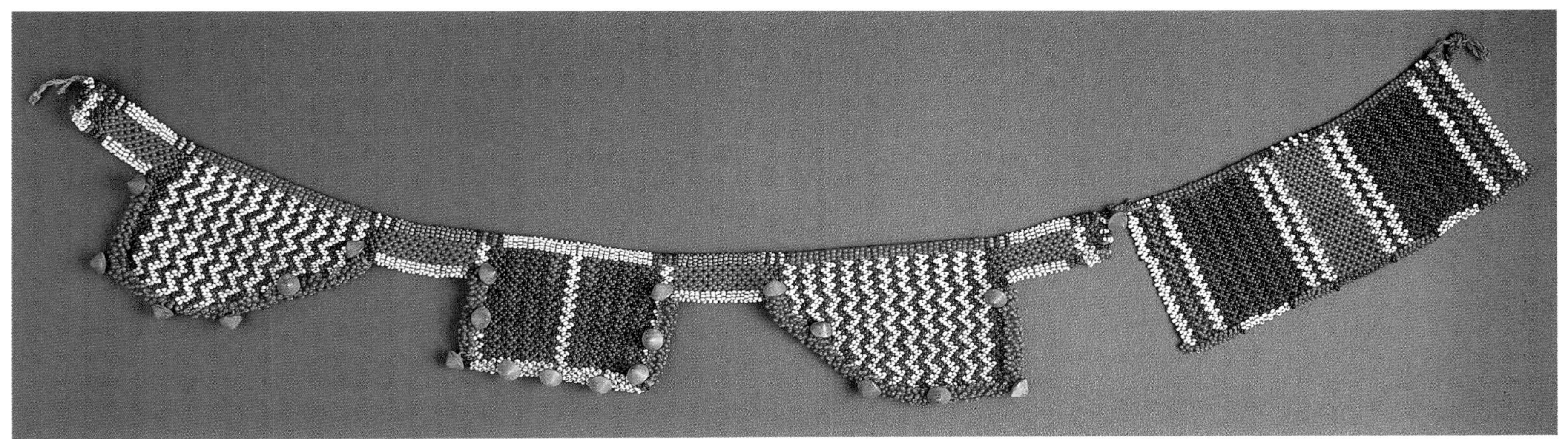

210

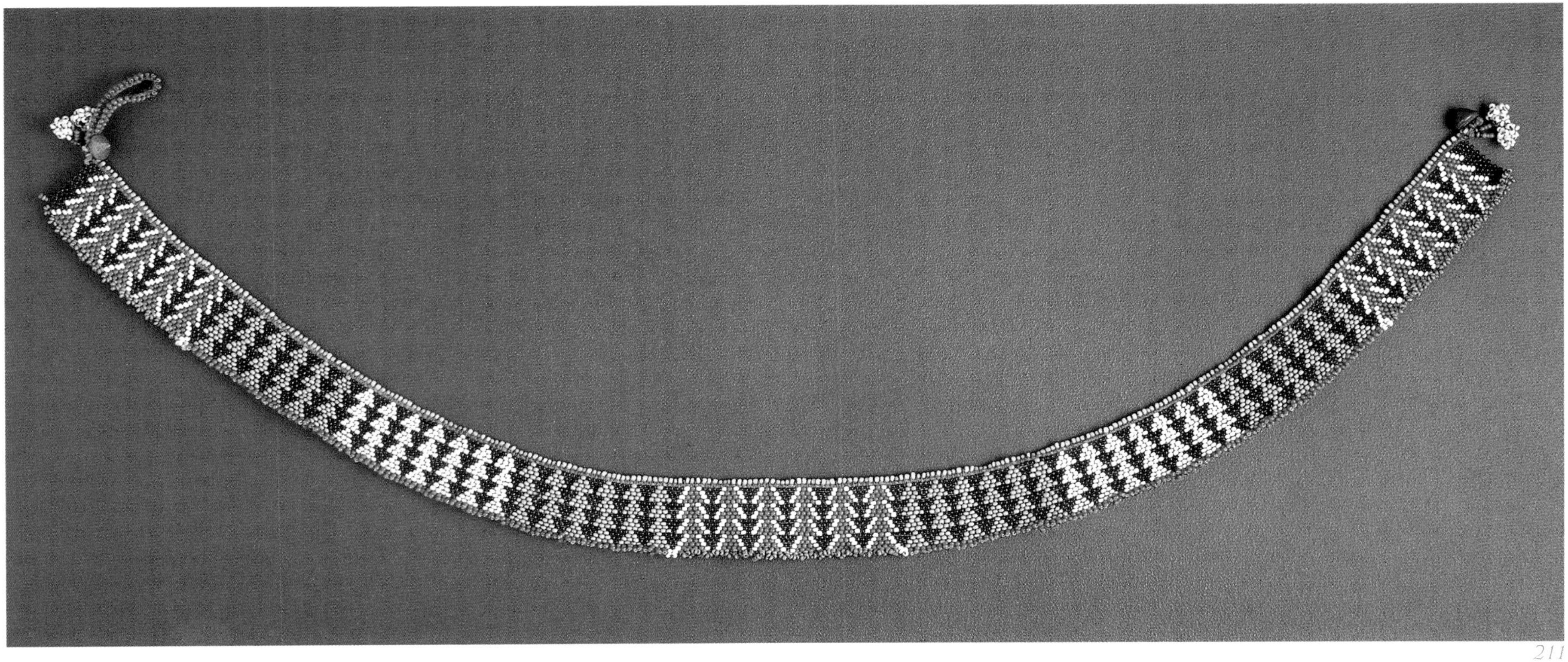

211

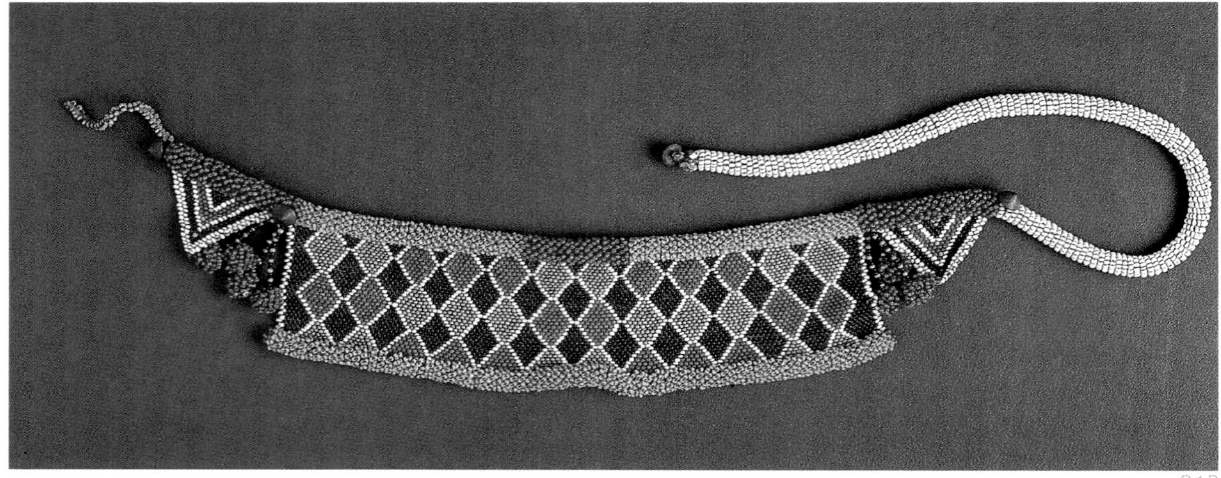

212

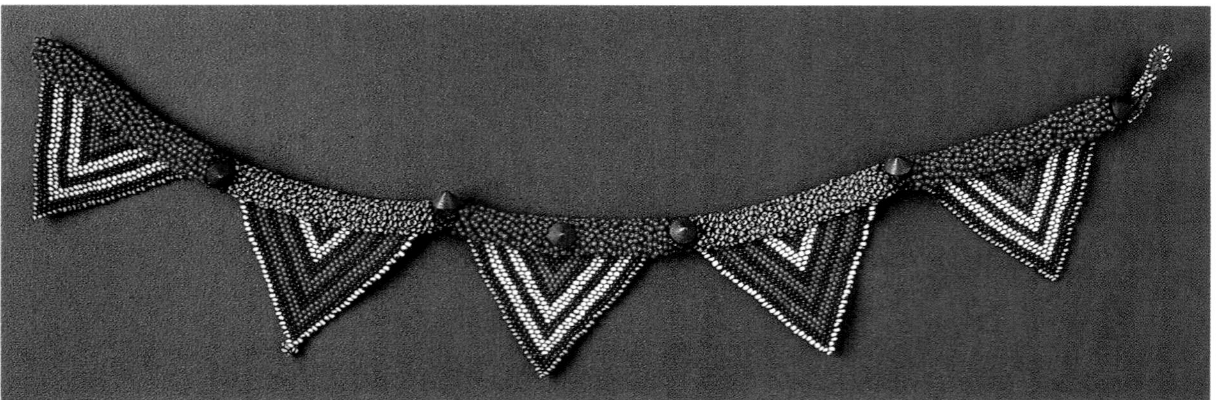

213

North Nguni
late 19th century

left:
212. Single-roll neckband with panel
panel: 30 x 8cm, length of band: 51cm
Provenance: Alfred John Gregory (1851–1927), who lived at the Cape between 1891 and 1914 and served as Medical Officer of Health for the Cape Colony between 1901 and 1910. See DSAB, vol. 5.
cf. *Zulu treasures*, Durban, 1986, B22.

213. Neckpiece
length: 59cm, triangles: 6 x 9cm each

right:
214. Waistband or bandolier
100 x 8cm

215. Waistband or bandolier
73 x 8cm

216. Neckband
50 x 5.5cm

See plate 15 for a late 19th-century photograph of a man wearing similar beadwork to nos. 214–216.

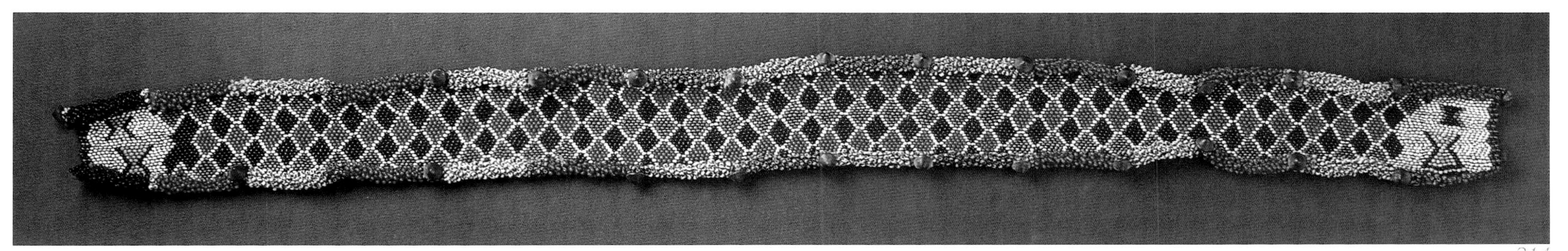

214

215

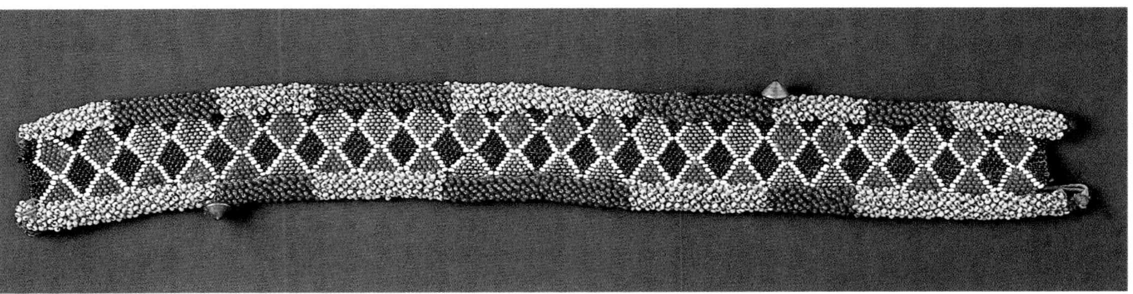

216

217

North Nguni
late 19th century

left:
217. Waistband or neckband with panel
panel: 10.5 x 15cm, length of strap: 65cm

right:
218. Fringed waistband with apron panel
panel: 13.5 x 22.5cm, overall length: 71cm

218

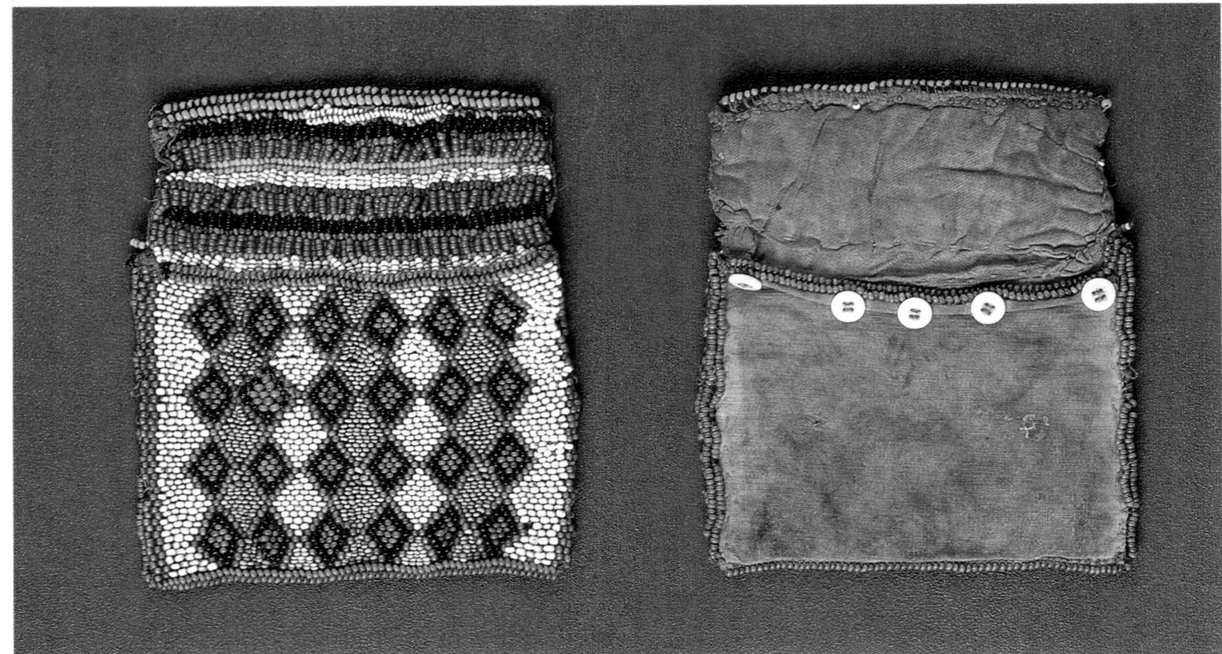

219

North Nguni
late 19th century

left:
219. Beaded cloth bag (front and back)
16 x 13.5cm

right:
220. Apron panel
15 x 24.5cm

cf. *Art and ambiguity*, Johannesburg, 1991, cat. no. 687.

220

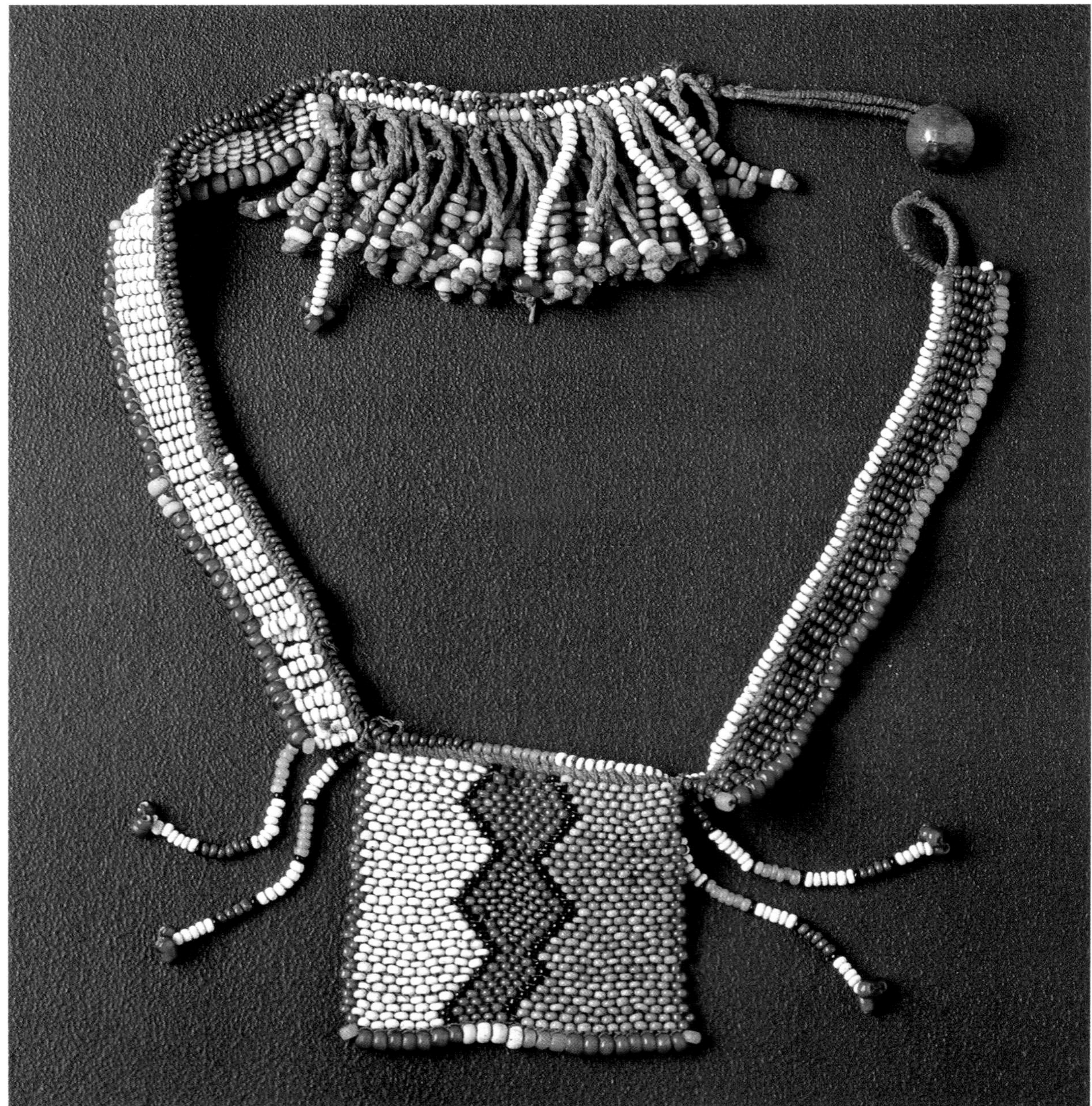

221

North Nguni
late 19th century

left:
221. Neckpiece
panel: 5 x 5.5cm

right:
222. Three-roll waistband with apron panel
panel: 9 x 18cm, waistband: 82 x 6cm

223. Three-roll waistband with apron panel
panel: 6.5 x 19cm, waistband: 70 x 3cm, with label 'From J. Fortuno / Direct Importers / Melmoth Zulu / ...'.

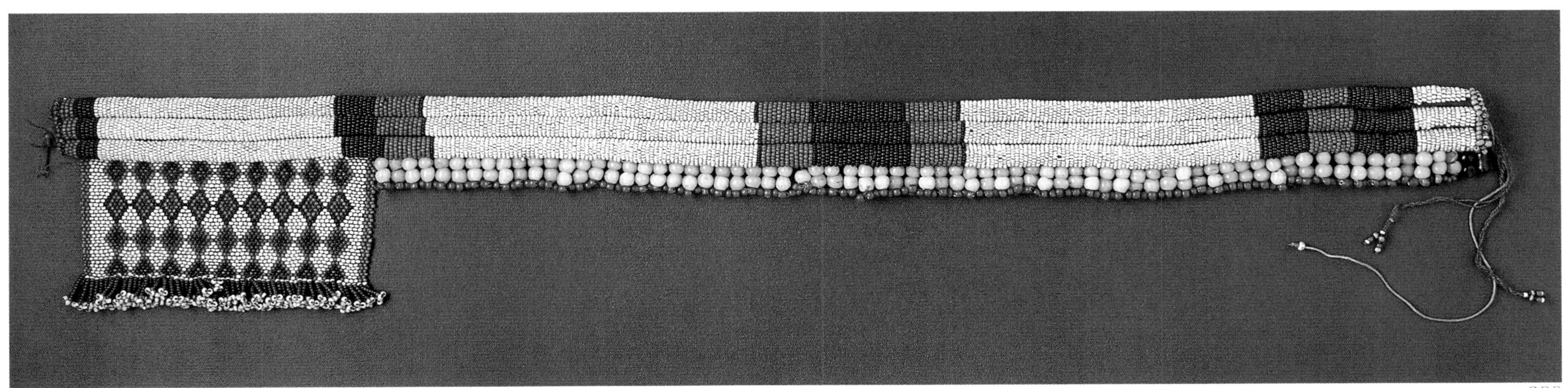

222

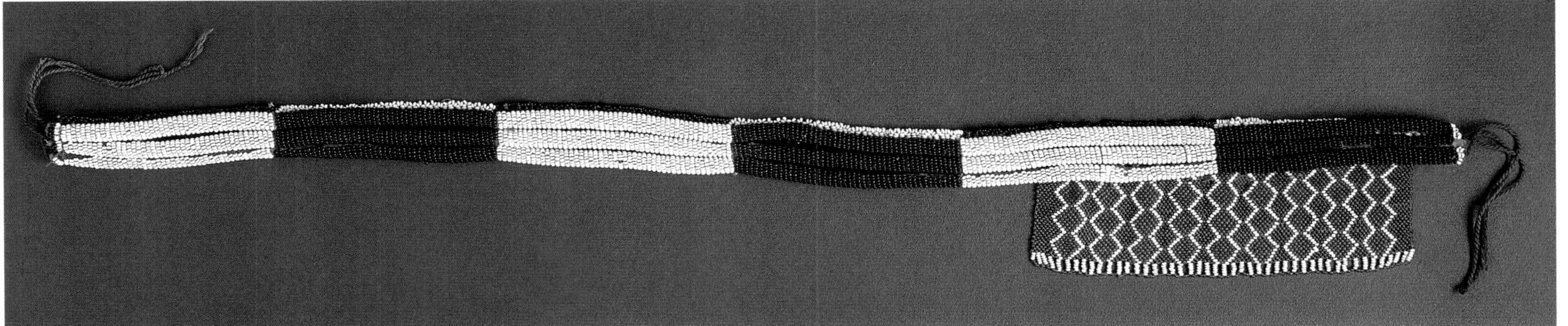

223

224

left:
224. North Nguni
Three-roll waistband and apron panel
late 19th century
panel: 41 x 28cm, waistband: 4.5 x 60cm

cf. *Art and ambiguity*, Johannesburg, 1991, cat. no. 672.

right:
225. North Nguni
Panel
late 19th century
12 x 34cm

following two pages:
left:
226. North Nguni
Beaded leather-backed waistband
late 19th century
79 x 5cm (excluding thongs)

227. North Nguni
Beaded leather-backed waistband
late 19th century
63 x 3.5cm (excluding thongs)

228. South-east Africa
Beaded cloth-backed waistband
late 19th century
78 x 8.5cm (excluding tassels)

right:
229. North Nguni
Beaded cloth-backed waistband
late 19th century
72.5 x 4.5cm

230. North Nguni
Waistband
late 19th century
62 x 6cm (excluding straps)

231. North Nguni
Beaded cloth-backed waistband
late 19th century
58 x 4.5cm (excluding straps)
with 19th-century label inscribed: 'The full dress uniform of a Zulu lady'

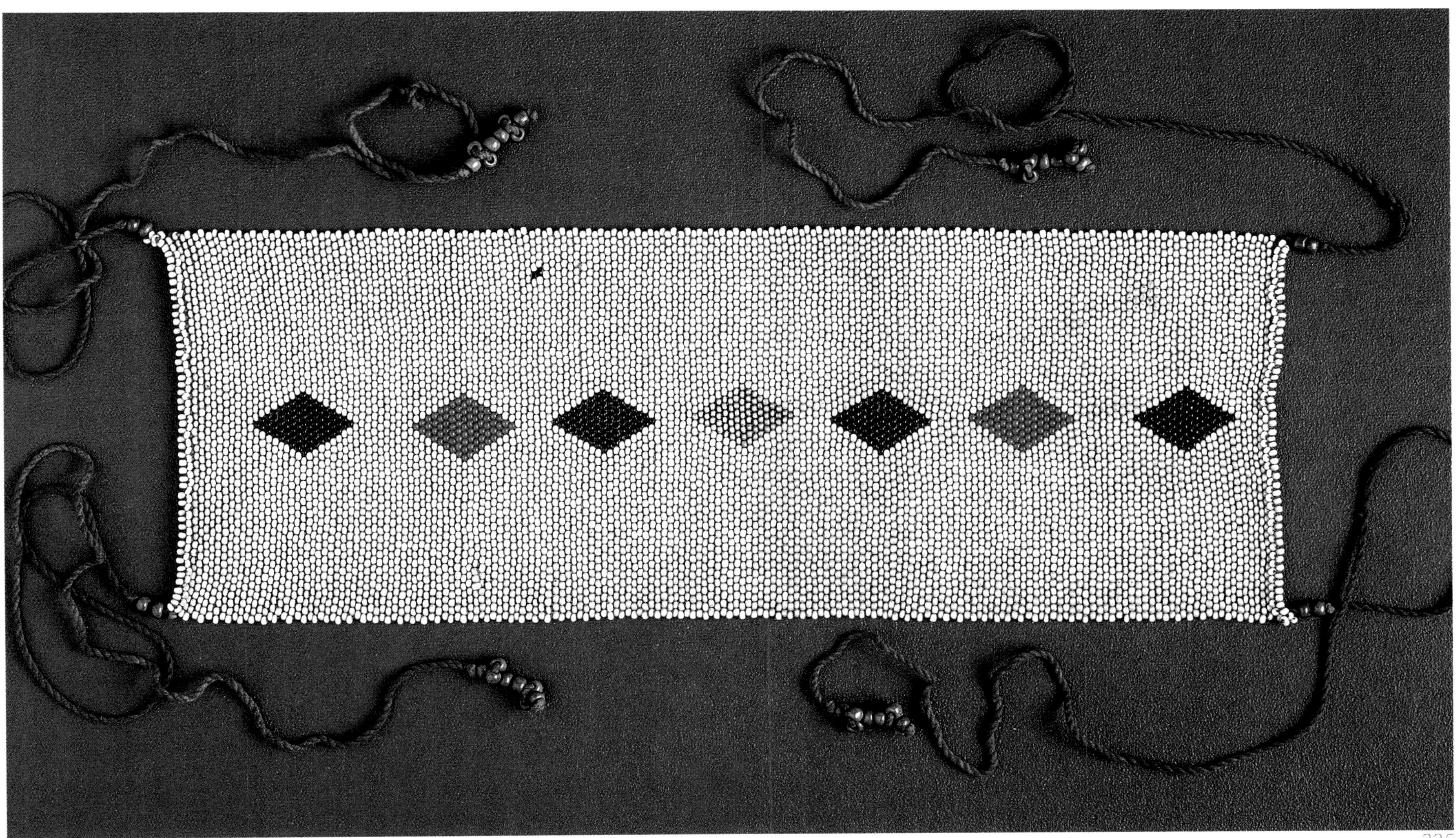

225

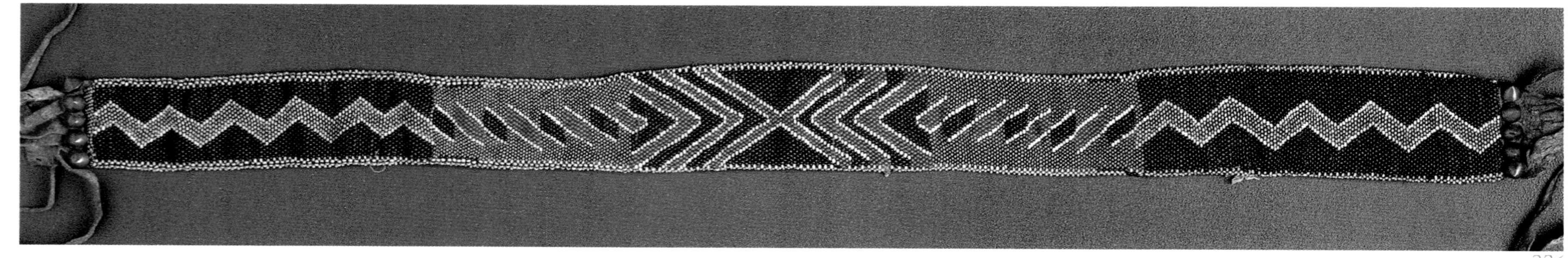

226

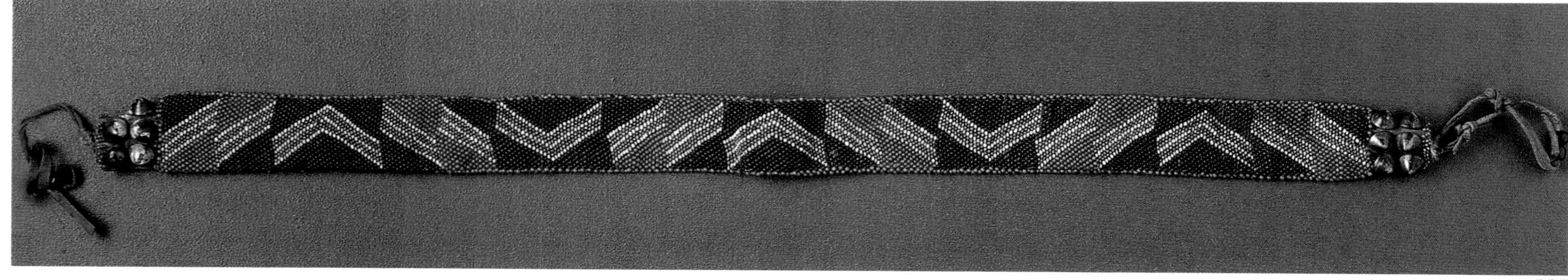

227

228

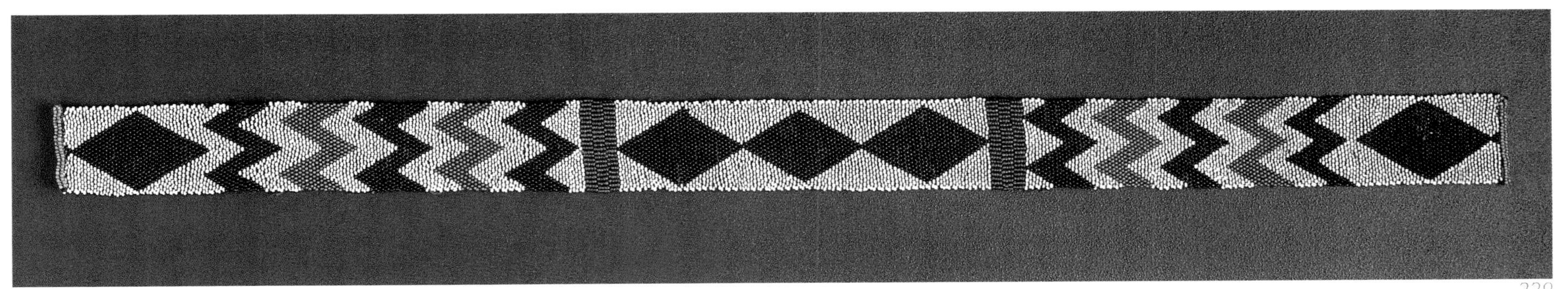

229

230

231

232

South-east Africa
late 19th century

left:
232. Beaded dagger and sheath
4 x 23cm

cf. *Zimbabwe: Legacies of stone*, Tervuren, 1997, vol. 1, p. 282.

right:
233. Beaded cloth-backed panel
17 x 57cm

233

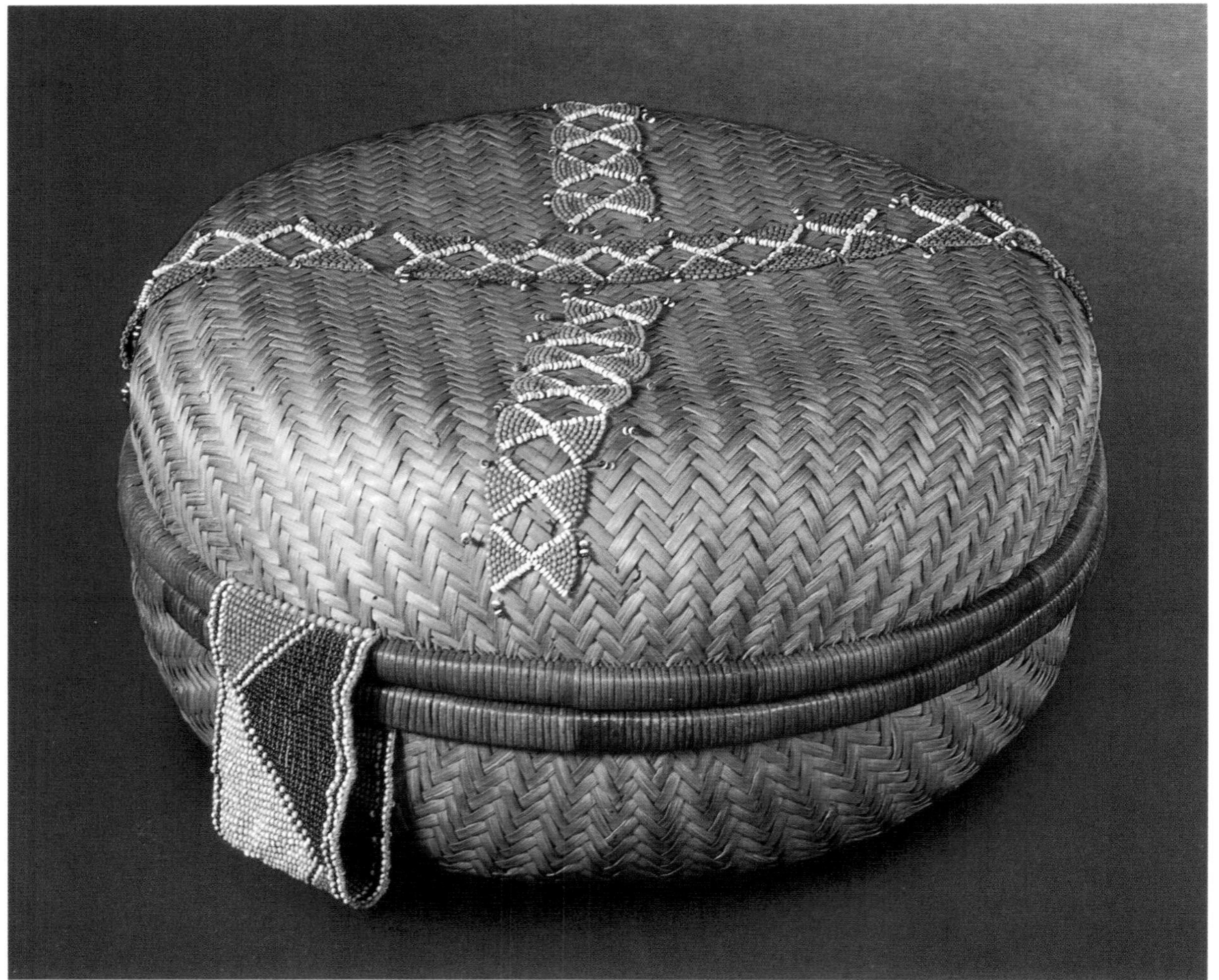

234

Eastern Zambezi region, probably Yao
late 19th century

left:
234. Beaded basket with cover attached with beaded strap
height: 18cm, width: 35.5cm

right:
235. Panel
26 x 79cm (excluding fringe)

following two pages:
Sashes

cf. M. Carey, *Beads and beadwork of East and South Africa*, 1986, p. 29; *Art and ambiguity*, Johannesburg, 1991, cat. nos. 740–742.

left:
236. *77 x 12.5cm*
237. *77 x 10cm*
238. *66 x 10cm*
239. *76 x 10cm*

right:
240. *67 x 12cm*
241. *79 x 9cm*
242. *66 x 12cm*
243. *66 x 6cm*

following two pages:
Sashes
left:
244. *81 x 13cm*
245. *77 x 6cm*
246. *77 x 8cm*
247. *77 x 7cm*

right:
248. *70 x 7cm*
249. *67.5 x 10cm*
250. *73 x 6.5cm*
251. *78 x 7.5cm*

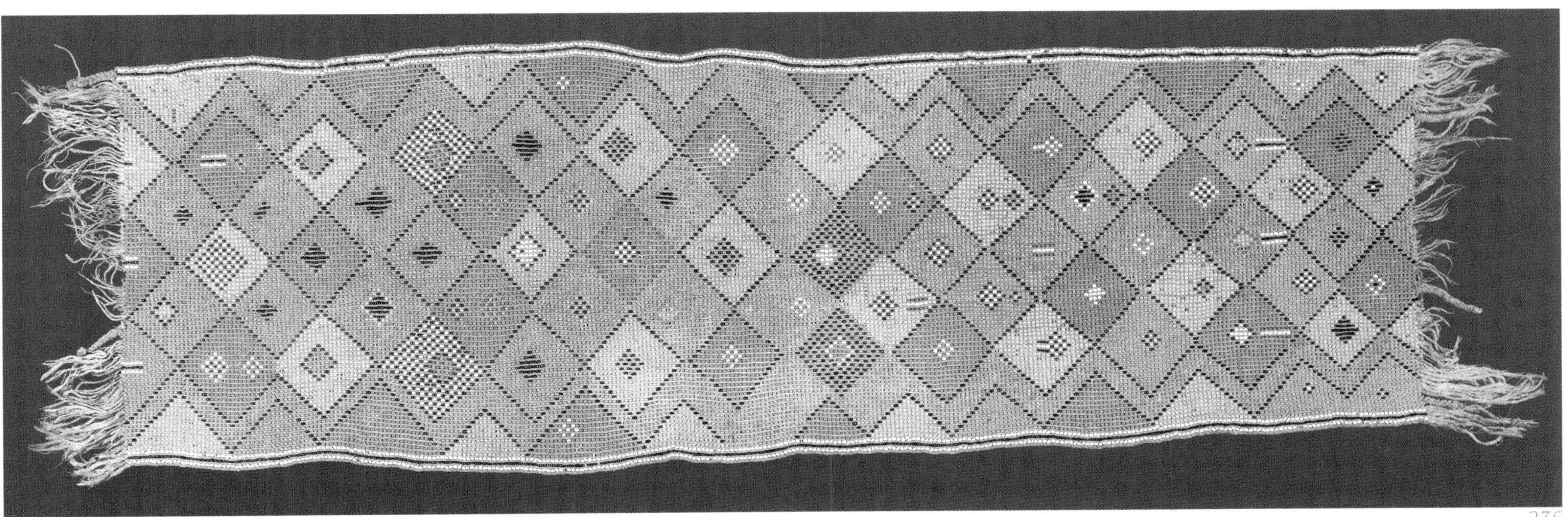

235

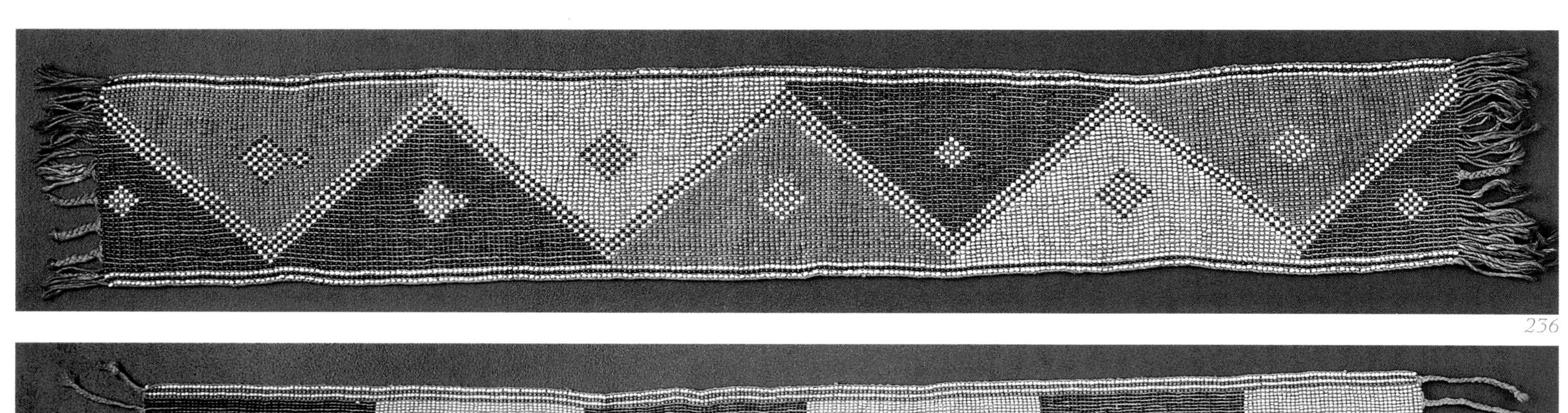

236

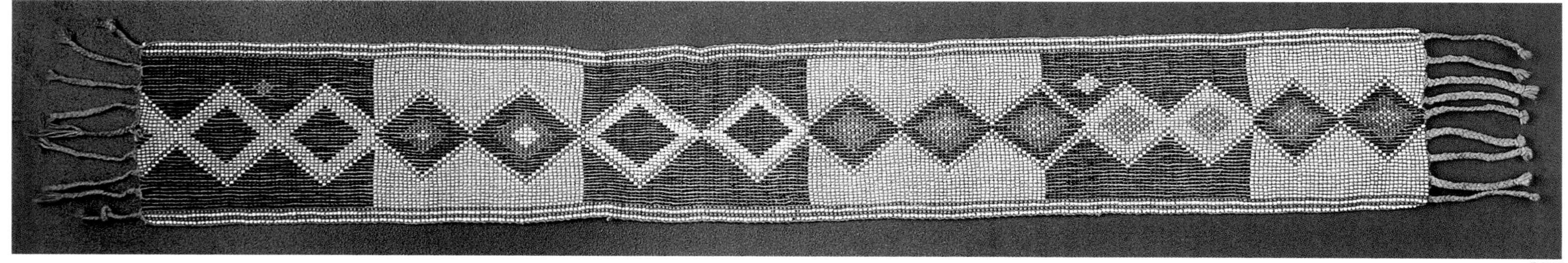

237

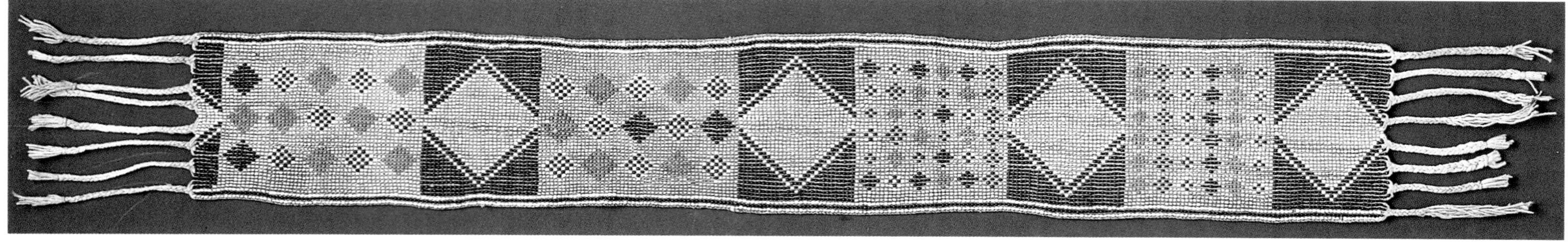

238

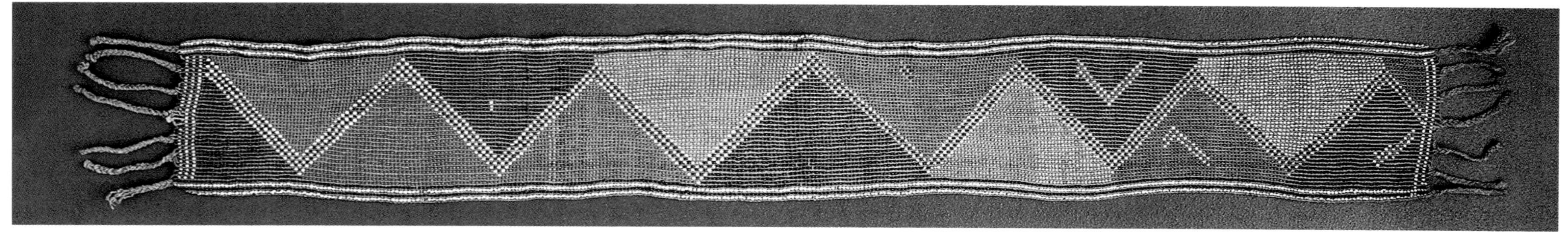

239

240

241

242

243

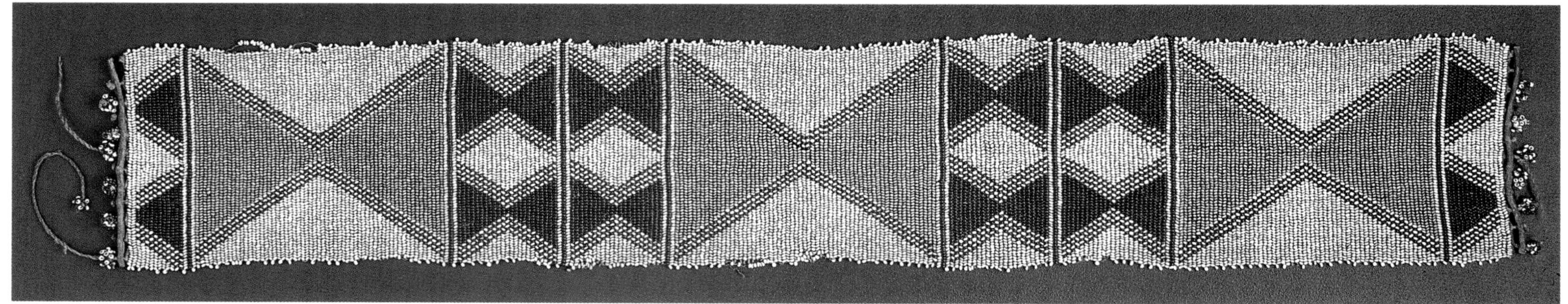

244

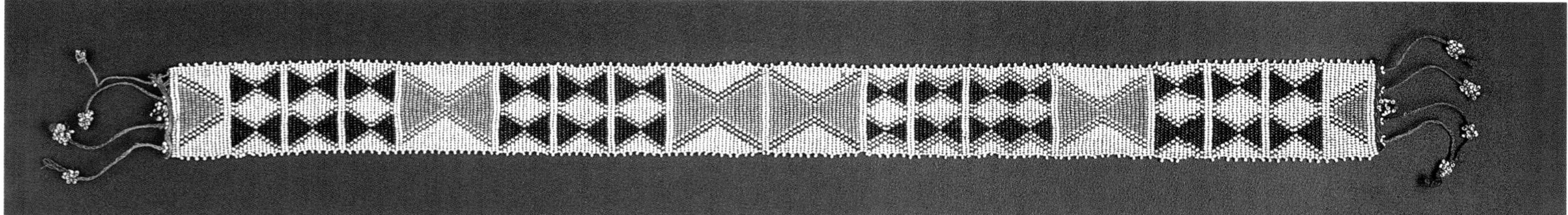

245

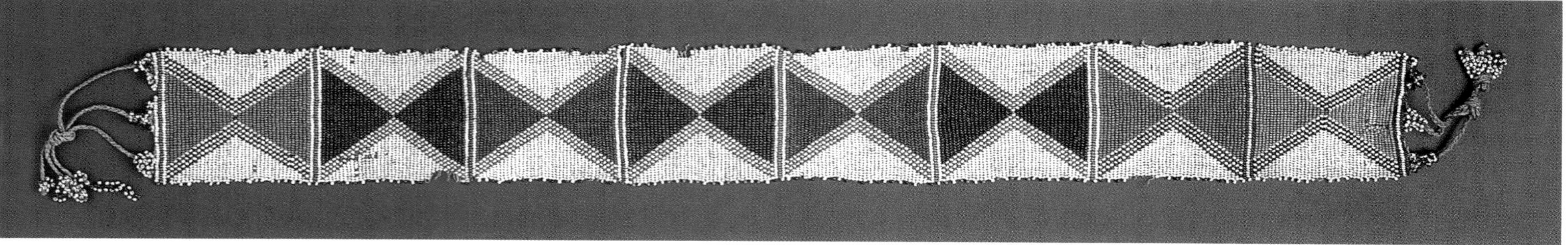

246

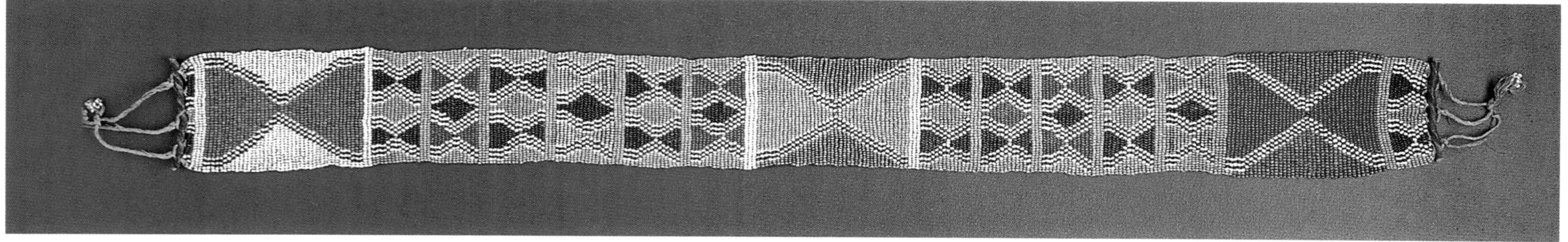

247

248

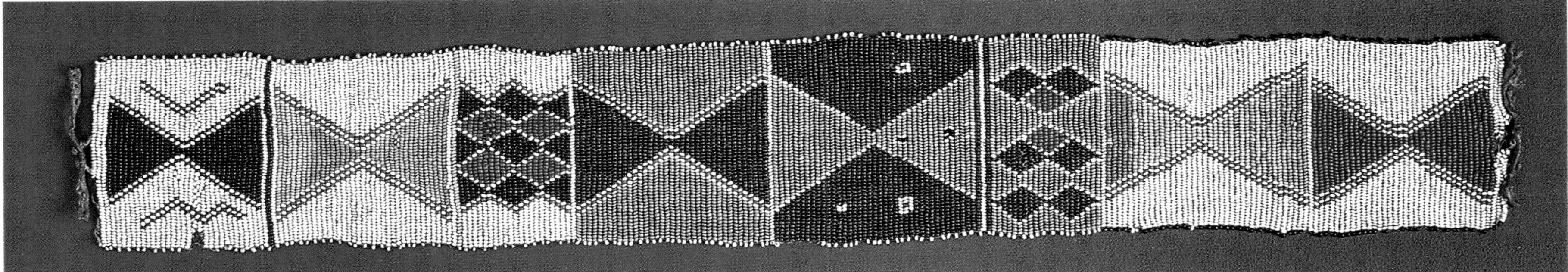

249

250

251

252, 253

254, 255, 256
257, 258, 259

Eastern Zambezi region, probably Yao

left:

Beaded reed combs
late 19th century

cf. M. Carey, *Beads and beadwork of East and South Africa*, 1986, p. 29; and H.P.N. Muller and J.F. Snelleman, *L'Industrie des Cafres du sud-est de l'Afrique*, c.1892, pl. XVI.

252. *10.6 x 6.5cm*
253. *10.1 x 6.4cm*
254. *12.6 x 7.9cm*
255. *11.5 x 8cm*
256. *12.5 x 8cm*
257. *8.6 x 6.9cm*
258. *12.2 x 14cm*
259. *10 x 7.6cm*

right:

260. Fringed apron panel
early 20th century
35 x 45.5cm

cf. M. Carey, *Beads and beadwork of East and South Africa*, 1986, p. 29; H.P.N. Muller and J.F. Snelleman, *L'Industrie des Cafres du sud-est de l'Afrique*, c.1892, pl. XIX(5).

260

261

262

263

264

Eastern Zambezi region

late 19th century

cf. the design and colours to H.P.N. Muller and J.F. Snelleman, *L'Industrie des Cafres du sud-est de l'Afrique*, c.1892, pl. XIX(5) described as 'Zambèze'.

left:

261. Beaded grass basket
height: 7cm, width: 14cm

262. Beaded glass bottle
height: 9cm

263. Beaded pouch
10 x 8cm

264. Beaded grass basket and cover
height: 5cm, width: 8.5cm

right:

265. Beaded grass basket and cover
height: 9cm, width: 21cm

265

266

Eastern Zambezi region, probably Yao

left:

266. Fringed apron panel
early 20th century
17.5 x 30cm

cf. M. Carey, *Beads and beadwork of East and South Africa*, 1986, p. 29.

right:

Sashes
late 19th century

267. *84 x 15cm*

268. *64.5 x 12.5cm*

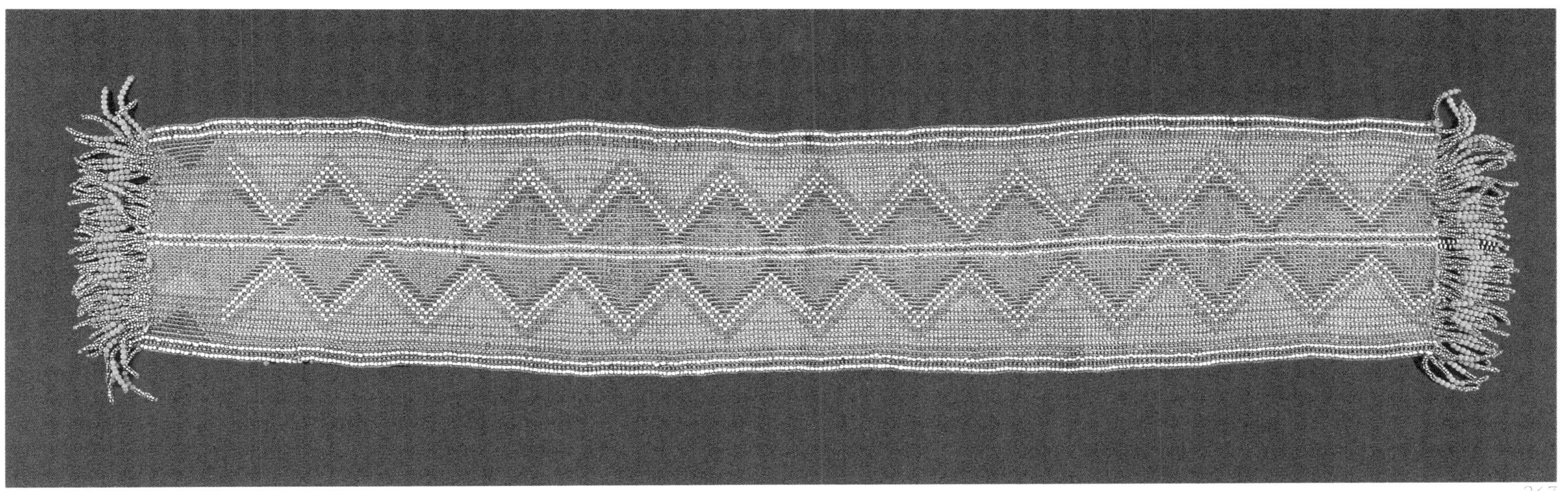

267

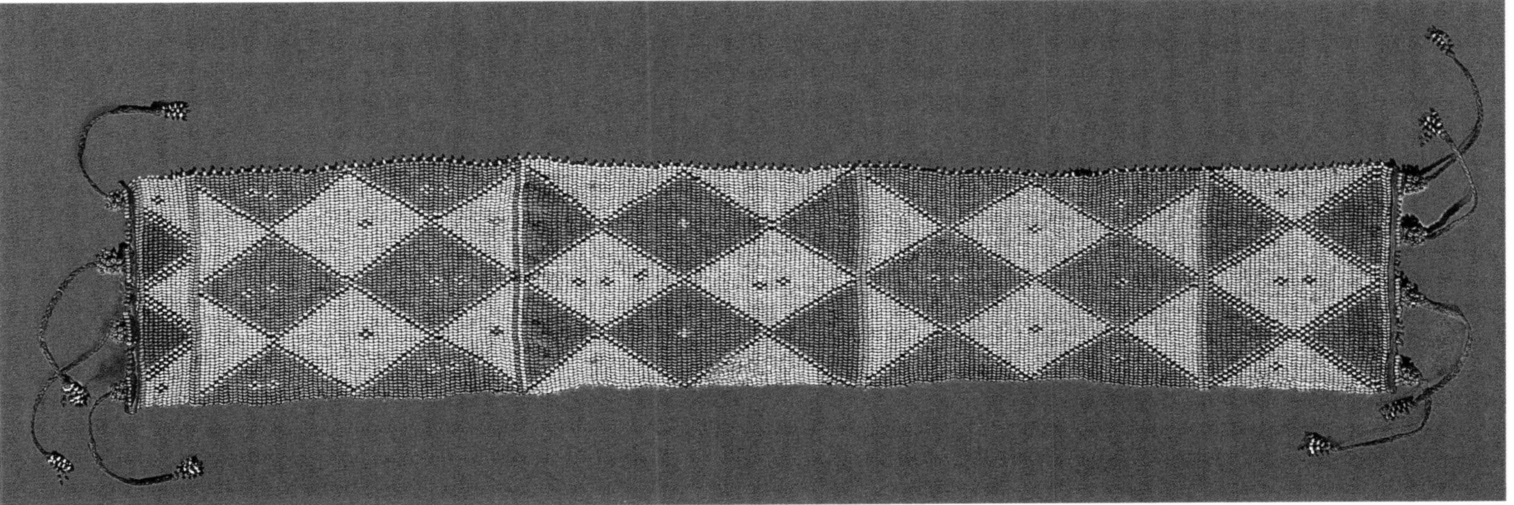

268

Endnotes

1. There is a wealth of literature on this process of transformation. Research done by Nettleton and Davison is especially interesting to this history in the southern African context. See, for example, A. Nettleton, '"... In what degree ... (they) are possessed of ornamental taste": A history of the writing on black art in South Africa'. In A. Nettleton and D. Hammond-Tooke, *African art in southern Africa. From tradition to township* (Johannesburg: A.D. Donker, 1989); A. Nettleton, 'Collections, exhibitions and histories: constructing a new South African art history'. In Butisitart, catalogue of the *Johannesburg Africus biennale* (Johannesburg: Transitional Metropolitan Council, 1995); and P. Davison, 'Ambiguity, style and meaning'. In *Art and ambiguity. Perspectives on the Brenthurst collection of southern African art* (Johannesburg: Johannesburg Art Gallery, 1991).

2. For a consideration of the Standard Bank collection of African art, see D. Hammond-Tooke and A. Nettleton (eds), *Ten years of collecting* (Johannesburg: University of the Witwatersrand, 1979).

3. The expedient political motivations possibly underlying the relocation in the early 1990s of beadwork from 'natural history' museums to galleries like the South African National Gallery in Cape Town are addressed by P. Davison in her article, 'Art as adornment: an ethnographic perspective'. In E. Bedford (ed.), *Ezakwantu: Beadwork from the eastern Cape* (Cape Town: South African National Gallery, 1993).

4. Davison makes this point very eloquently in 'Art as adornment: an ethnographic perspective'.

5. H.J. Bruce, 'The arts and crafts of the Transvaal Ndebele'. In A.H. Smith (ed.), *Africana byways* (Johannesburg: A.D. Donker, 1976) and N. Knight and S. Priesbach, 'Traditional Ndebele beadwork', *African Arts*, 11(2), January 1978.

6. This history is discussed at length by E.A. Schneider in her unpublished PhD thesis, *Paint, pride and politics: aesthetic meaning in Transvaal Ndebele wall art* (Johannesburg: University of the Witwatersrand, 1987) and by P. Delius, 'The Ndzundza Ndebele: Indenture and the making of ethnic identity'. In P. Bonner (et al), *Holding their ground: class, locality and culture in nineteenth- and twentieth-century South Africa* (Johannesburg: Ravan Press and the University of the Witwatersrand Press, 1989).

7. See D. Levy, *Continuities and change in Ndebele beadwork: 1883 to the present* (unpublished MA dissertation, Johannesburg: University of the Witwatersrand, 1990).

8. Archaeological evidence pointing to the use of beads in what was later to become the Zulu kingdom is discussed by M. Hall and T.M. Maggs in their article, 'Nqubeni: A later iron age site in Zululand', *South African Archaeological Bulletin*, Goodwin Series, 3:159–176, 1979.

9. See N. Etherington, 'The "Shepstone system" in the Colony of Natal and beyond the border'. In A. Duminy and B. Guest (eds), *Natal and Zululand from earliest times to 1910. A new history* (Pietermaritzburg: University of Natal Press and Shuter and Shooter, 1989).

10. J.B. Wright and C. Hamilton, 'Traditions and transformations: the Phongola-Mzimkhulu region in the late eighteenth and early nineteenth centuries'. In A. Duminy and B. Guest (eds), *Natal and Zululand from earliest times to 1910. A new history* (Pietermaritzburg: University of Natal Press and Shuter and Shooter, 1989) and C. Hamilton and J.B. Wright, 'The making of the amaLala. Ethnicity, ideology and relations of subordination in a precolonial context', *Southern African Historical Journal*, 22, 1990.

11. S. Klopper, '"A man of splendid appearance": Angas's *Utimuni*, nephew of the late king, Chaka', *African Studies*, 54(1), 1994.

12. This collection is discussed in B.V. Brottem and A. Lang, 'Zulu beadwork', *African Arts*, 6:8–13, 64, 83–84, 1973.

13. See Klopper, 'A man of splendid appearance'.

14. On the subject of these shows, see especially R.D. Altick's now classic 1978 study, *The shows of London* (Cambridge, Massachusetts: Belknap Press of Harvard University Press).

15. See, for example, W. Worger, 'Clothing dry bones: The myth of Shaka', *Journal of African Studies*, Fall 1979 and C. Hamilton, *Terrific Majesty* (Cape Town: David Philip, 1997).

16. S. Klopper, 'George French Angas' (re)presentation of the Zulu in *The kafirs illustrated*', *South African Journal of Cultural and Art History*, 3(1), 1989.

17. Altick, *The shows of London*, 282f.

18. S.J.R. Martin, *British images of the Zulu c.1820–1879* (unpublished PhD, Cambridge University, 1982).

19. There are several important exceptions to this tendency, most notably the collection assembled by Major Clem Webb c.1880. Significantly, though, Webb was born in the eastern Cape. His interest in the beadwork of Xhosa-speaking communities therefore developed through long-term personal interaction with the people from whom he acquired this collection.

20. See, for example, the artefacts acquired by the Austrian-Hungarian consul in Port Elizabeth in 1873. B. Plankensteiner, *Austusch. Kunst aus dem südlichen Afrika um 1900* (Vienna: Museum fur Völkerkunde, 1998).

21. H.A. Junod, *The life of a South African tribe*, 2 volumes (New York: University Books Inc., 1962), vol. 1:275.

22. Junod, *The Life of a South African tribe*, vol. 2:103.

23. There is a wealth of African beadwork in the Overseas Museum of Ethnology in Lisbon but, according to Rayda Becker, most of this beadwork is not provenanced. In many cases, it is not even clear whether the beadwork from southern Africa housed in this museum was collected in Angola or Mozambique.

24. These Swiss collections are discussed in considerable detail by R. Becker in her unpublished PhD thesis, *Tsonga headrests: the making of an art history category* (University of the Witwatersrand, 1999).

25. E.A. Alpers, *Ivory and slaves in east central Africa. Changing patterns of international trade in the later nineteenth century* (London: Heinemann, 1975).

26. Generally speaking Yao beadwork is mentioned only in passing, as in M. Carey, *Beads and beadwork of East and South Africa* (London: Shire Publications, 1986).

27. R. Summers, unpublished manuscript, 'A note on the bead trade in southern and south-eastern Africa', cited in M. Hall, *The changing past: farmers, kings and traders in southern Africa, 200–1860* (Cape Town: David Philip, 1987), 79.

28. Some of these indigenous materials are discussed in P. Mayr, 'Language of colours amongst the Zulu expressed by their bead-work ornaments; and some general notes on their personal adornments and clothing', *Annals of the Natal Museum*, 2, 1907:159–165.

29. S. Bourquin (ed.), *Paulina Dlamini. Servant of two kings*. Compiled by H. Filter (Durban and Pietermaritzburg: Killie Campbell Africana Library and Natal University Press, 1986), 38.

30. C. Kaufmann, 'The bead rush: developments in the nineteenth-century bead trade from Cape Town to King William's Town'. In E. Bedford (ed.), *Ezakwantu. Beadwork from the eastern Cape* (Cape Town: South African National Gallery, 1993). Some of this history is also discussed in C. Crais, *The making of the colonial order. White supremacy and black resistance in the eastern Cape, 1770–1865* (Johannesburg: University of the Witwatersrand, 1992).

31. M. Shaw and N.J. van Warmelo, 'The material culture of the Cape Nguni, Part 4, Personal and General', *Annals of the South African Museum*, 58(4), 1988, 868.

32. R.B. Beck, 'Bibles and beads: missionaries as traders in southern Africa in the early nineteenth century', *Journal of African History*, 30, 1989.

33. G.E. Cory (ed.), *The diary of the Rev. Francis Owen* (Cape Town: The Van Riebeeck Society, 1926), 25.

34. N. Isaacs, *Travels and adventures in Africa*, 2 volumes (Cape Town: The Van Riebeeck Society, 1936), vol. 2, 284.

35. P.R. Kirby (ed.), *Andrew Smith and Natal. Documents relating to the early history of that province* (Cape Town: The Van Riebeeck Society, 1955), 32.

36. J. Stuart and D. Mck Malcolm (eds), *The diary of Henry Francis Fynn* (Pietermaritzburg: Shuter and Shooter, 1969), 158–59.

37. D.K. Rycroft and A.B. Ngobo (eds), *The praises of Dingana. Izibongo zikaDingana* (Durban and Pietermaritzburg: Killie Campbell Africana Library and University of Natal Press, 1988), 4.

38. G.F. Angas, *The Kafirs illustrated* (London: Hogarth 1849), 55.

39. Cory, *The diary of the Rev. Francis Owen*, 61.

40. Stuart and Malcolm, *The diary of Henry Francis Fynn*, 5.

41. A. Gardiner, *Narrative of a journey to the Zoolu country* (London: William Crofts, 1836), 169.

42. J. Bird (ed.), *The annals of Natal, 1495–1845* (Cape Town: C. Struik, reprint edition, 1965), 205.

43. Gardiner, *Journey to the Zoolu country*, 39.

44. Bird, *Annals*, 205.

45. Cory, *The diary of the Rev. Francis Owen*, 50.

46. Angas, *The Kafirs illustrated*, 87.

47. C. Barter, *Alone among the Zulus* (Durban and Pietermaritzburg: Killie Campbell Africana Library and Natal University Press, 1995), 119, 121.

48. Kirby, *Andrew Smith and Natal*, 32.

49. O.H. Spohr (ed.), *The Natal diaries of Dr W.H.I. Bleek, 1855–1856* (Cape Town: A.A. Balkema, 1965), 74–5.

50. A. Nettleton et al., 'The beadwork of the Cape Nguni'. In D. Hammond-Tooke and A. Nettleton (eds), *Ten years of collecting* (Johannesburg: University of the Witwatersrand Press, 1989), 40.

51. A-I. Berglund, *Zulu thought-patterns and symbolism* (Cape Town: David Philip, 1976), 161.

52. Berglund, *Zulu thought-patterns*, 130.

53. Four volumes of these oral histories have been published so far by the Killie Campbell Africana Library and the University of Natal Press.

54. W.R. Ludlow, *Zululand and Cetewayo* (London: Simpkins, Marshall and Co., 1882), 78.

55. J.W. Colenso, *Ten weeks in Natal* (Cambridge: MacMillan, 1855), 30.

56. C. Hamilton, 'Women and material markers of identity'. In E. Dell (ed.), *Evocations of the child. Fertility figures of the southern African region* (Cape Town: Human and Rousseau, n.d.), 23.

57. See footnote 56. Although this collection of essays seems to have no publication date, it first appeared in 1998.

58. P. Harries, 'The roots of ethnicity: discourse and the politics of language construction in south-east Africa', *African Affairs* 87(346), 1988.

59. Becker, *Tsonga headrests*.

60. Considerable attention has been devoted to developing a better understanding of the kinds of alliances 19th-century communities are likely to have formed. In this regard, see especially W.D. Hammond-Tooke, 'Descent groups, chiefdoms and South African historiography', *Journal of Southern African Studies*, 11(2), April 1985, 305–319 and A. Kuper, *The invention of primitive society. Transformations of an illusion* (London: Routledge, 1988).

61. A.M. Duggan-Cronin, *The bantu tribes of South Africa. The Vathonga*, Vol. IV, Section 1. Introduction and notes by H.P. Junod (Cambridge: Deighton Bell, 1939), 13.

62. H. Friedman, 'Ntwane gimwane. Ntwane grass figures'. In *Evocations of the child*, 131.

63. Davison, 'Adornment as art', 24.

64. Shaw and van Warmelo, 'The material culture of the Cape Nguni', 485.

65. C. de B. Webb and J.B. Wright (eds), *The James Stuart Archive*, vol. 1 (Durban and Pietermaritzburg: Killie Campbell Library and University of Natal Press, 1976), 322–3.

66. Bourquin, *Paulina Dlamini*, 36.

67. Mayr, 'Language of colours amongst the Zulu' and N. Woods, 'Zulu beadwork'. In *Zulu treasures: of kings and commoners* (Durban: KwaZulu Cultural Museum and the Local History Museums, 1996).

68. See L. Hooper, 'The social life of beads: expressive uses of beadwork in the eastern Cape'. In E. Bedford (ed.), *Ezakwantu. Beadwork from the eastern Cape* (Cape Town: South African National Gallery, 1993).

69. S. Klopper, 'Women's work, or engendering the art of beadwork in southern Africa'. In Bedford, *Ezakwantu*.

70. H.L. Moore, *Feminism and anthropology* (Cambridge: Polity Press, 1988), 68–70.

71. Hooper, 'The social life of beads'.

72. M. Buthelezi in a speech delivered at the Lidchi Gallery in Johannesburg, 21 November 1979. These and other speeches by the former Chief Minister of KwaZulu are available from the archives of the University of South Africa in Pretoria.

73. Buthelezi, Lidchi Gallery speech, 21 November 1979.

74. On this subject see S. Klopper, '"I respect custom, but I am not a tribalist": The ANC, the Congress of Traditional Leaders and designer tradition', *South African Journal of Historical Studies*, 39, 1988.

75. Some of this history is addressed in S. Klopper, 'Re-dressing the past: the Africanisation of sartorial style in contemporary South Africa'. In A. Brah and A. Coombes (eds), *From miscegenation to hybridity* (London: Routledge, 2000).

76. See, for example, the final chapter in E. Preston-Whyte, *Speaking with beads. Zulu art from southern Africa* (London: Thames and Hudson, 1994).

Index

detail, Zulu Portraits Album, *c. 1890*.
Photograph: National Library of S.A., Cape Town

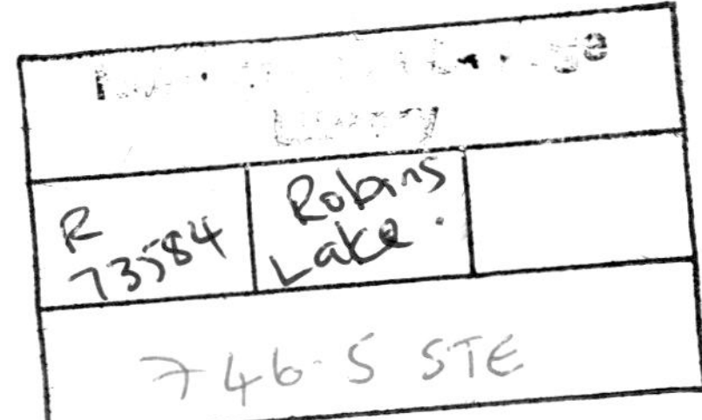